A SPECIAL
PLACE IN
HELL

A SPECIAL PLACE IN HELL

THE WORLD'S MOST DEPRAVED SERIAL KILLERS

CHRISTOPHER BERRY-DEE

First published in 2021 by Ad Lib Publishers Ltd
15 Church Road
London, SW13 9HE

www.adlibpublishers.com

Text © 2021 Christopher Berry-Dee

ISBN 978-1-913543-75-4
eBook ISBN 978-1-913543-69-3
ISBN 978-1-786751-21-8

A CIP catalogue record for this book is available from the
British Library.
Every reasonable effort has been made to trace copy-
right-holders of material reproduced in this book, but if
any have been inadvertently overlooked the publishers
would be glad to hear from them.

Printed in the UK
10 9 8 7 6 5 4 3 2 1

With fond memories of my dear late friend and colleague, Peter Aldred who passed away in Manila, April 2020

Contents

Acknowledgements

Phew! Oh, where do I start here? But of course it has to start with my wife, Claire, and my son, Jack; an incredible mother, and a beautiful boy all supported by her parents, Trevor and Carol who are always here for me as I am for them. Then there is my sister, Lizzie, Jim and all of Clan Stothard.

So many close friends have been with me and supported me throughout many of the books I have written: my mentor Robin Odell; Clive Study former RN – now a pilot with Lincs and Notts Air Ambulance; fellow author Boris Coster at www.broadmoorsinister.com; Steve McCullough; Laurel Lee from Chicago, Illinois; George Arm; Sam and Mark Adrian Hayes WOII RM; my great web designer Luke Thompson from Georgia; my long-time colleague-in-arms TV producer Frazer Ashford; Martin Mahoney aka 'Mr Le Creuset' (sponsor of charity shops) UK-wide. Mandi Fenwick; Jenny Wiseman former WRN; Roy Haywood; Julie Mainstone; Jennie Tinkler; Claire-Louise; Jan Fuller; Mhairi Lyn; Robert Pothecary; Kelly-Marie Turner; the incorrigible Rod Crowshaw; Linda Newcombe; Jade Muirhead; Cynthia and

Christopher Grist; Amy Lock; Gary and Anita Roberts; Jason Thorley; Gary Bone; Neil Robert Scullion; Emma Preston; Immy; Jon Sotnick; Wilfie Cummings; Martin Mc – former RN; Liam Greavey; Dave Uppal; Murat Harman; former Miss World Ann Sidney; Karl Spencer-Smith; Simone from the Philippines as are Romelyn, the adorable Chie and Dja.

Yep, I guess that's that bit done and dusted, so now to my colleagues: TVS; Ray Pedretti at Blizzard Road Productions; Ric at Monster Films; WH Smith booksellers; Waterstones; my Russian Federation publishers 'ESKMO'; Adam Podlewski at my Polish publishers CZARNA OWCA; my US publishers Ulysses; Shaun Attwood at Spiral Studios; Gemma Day Photography; the *Mirror*; *Daily Mail*; *Daily Express*; *The Times*; BBC; ITV; the FBI; John Blake and Jon Rippon at Ad Lib Publishing, and all of my colleagues at John Blake/Bonnier UK; Tara Lawrence at CNN/HLN; Shereen Low, celebrity writer at *True Crime Monthly* and *Horzu Wissen*; Kelly Weeks Marketing Studio and Ashley Meikle; Christine Hart; Rick Mayston at FOX MEDIA, NY; Vicky Bray at ZNACTV; Patrick Hill – *Sunday Mirror*; Alba A. Proko (Product Manager, e-Book, Audio & Apps) Bonnier Books UK and actor Colin Mace who narrated my international bestsellers into CDs: *Talking with Psychopaths and Savages: Beyond Evil*, and, *Talking with Serial Killers: A Chilling Study of the World's Most Evil People*. Numerous law enforcement officers and agencies in the UK, USA, the St Petersburg State Police. Police Major Gideon Aynsjr; Det. Sgt Ronald Villagranda. CIDG – Homicide, Makati Central Police Station, Manila.

Finally those who have made my trips overseas such an enjoyable experience: Justin Gerard L. Agus – Manager Oxford Suites Hotel, Makati, Manila; R-Mar Resort & Spa, Patong, Kathu, Phuket, Thailand; all the staff at Café Cubana, Makati; Joanna Hannah Teh, MBE, Vice Consul, British Embassy, Manila; Emirates – who give the best Business Class service in the world – and my travel agent, Ajay at Southall Travel.

Foreword

'At the bottom of the abyss there is unimaginable suffering, screaming and pain.'
From the 2018 horror/thriller Mandy *starring Nicolas Cage*

I'll be honest with my readers and say that I didn't select the title, *A Special Place In Hell: The World's Most Depraved Serial Killers* – oh, no, my publishers did the picking and left me to do the rest. I mean, c'mon guys, you've just managed thirteen words and I have got to put together at least 75,000 more of well thought out, informative material to keep you, my intensely loyal readers, on the edge of your seats for God knows how many pages. And guess what? John Blake and Jon Rippon could not even give me a shortlist of figures they think qualify for inclusion.

I'll tell you what this is – it's a damned impertinence if you care to ask my opinion. Laziness, that's what it is! However, as some of you might know, I have interviewed, face-to-face, some thirty serial killers, mass and one-off murderers and I've corresponded with countless more, clearing up a few cold cases on my way, so I guess I am qualified to write *something* about some of the worst serial killers of all time. As for Hell – well, I haven't been there – not just yet – but with the way things are going right now, those pearly gates surrounded by pert little angels with feathery wings seem a distant dream simply because the only Christmas cards I get are from monsters behind bars.

One has to consider the nature of 'Hell'. It is a place regarded in various religions as a spiritual realm of evil and suffering. It is traditionally depicted as a place of perpetual fire beneath the earth where the wicked are punished after death. Therefore, to give you value for money, I plucked this from my Holy Bible – not a personally signed first edition please understand!

But as for the cowardly, the faithless, the detestable,
as for murderers, the sexually immoral, and all liars,
their portion will be in the lake that burns with fire and
sulfur, which is the second death.

Revelation 21:8

This 'Mr Revelation' certainly had a bee in his bonnet about this as he added this too:

And the smoke of their torment goes up forever and ever, and
they have no rest, day or night, these worshippers of the beast
and its image, and whoever receives the mark of its name.

Revelation 14:11

Of course, that is *not* the be-all and end-all of it, because Messrs: Thessalonians; Matthew; Peter; Jude; John; Mark; Luke and some Romans all have their own take on what awaits sinners in Hell. To my mind, visiting this place called 'Hell' would be like being flung into the most dangerous volcano on earth when it's having a bad day – I'm picturing Mount Vesuvius blowing its top in the catastrophic eruption of 79 AD that destroyed the Roman city of Pompeii. Now, that's what I call being up 'Larva Shit Creek' without a paddle, if I say so myself.

Yet, here are my publishers commissioning me to go to this God awful place and meet the ten most evil serial killers who have a 'special place' there. Maybe they have some sort of executive suite reserved only for the highest class of monsters?

The other issues that concerned me as I tried to comprehend *any* of the twenty-nine-page commissioning agreement impatiently awaiting signature on my desk in front of me were as follows:

1: The humble advance made no mention of any expenses I might incur while travelling to and from this place called 'Hell'. No insurance policy for the very real chance of fire damage, either. That's a damned cheek, if you care to ask me.

2: Clause iiiB3 on page six, sub-section 572, stated 'We, the publishers, will sue you post-mortem and take everything you ever had, have or would be likely to have had, if you fail to complete the aforementioned text to our total satisfaction and let the Devil take the hindmost'.

3: Then on page thirteen, sub-section 829, clause xxxiiix Y10: 'Now bugger off and find the ten most evil serial killers on earth and *you* choose which ones will make the cut.'

On a more serious note – simply because sado-sexual serial homicide *is* an extremely *serious* subject – it rather boils down to one's own personal perspective when you are asked to name the very worst of this murderous ilk. For most westerners who have a thing about criminology and these serial life-takers, usually the first name that hits the top of the list is Theodore 'Ted' Robert Bundy (1946–1989). This may seem a bitter pill to swallow but, in the sad theme of things, he wasn't actually a big hitter as far as these types of monsters go. Yes, he confessed thirty sexually sadistic kills, the total is unconfirmed – it could be more, it could be less – and yes, he *was* what some may call 'handsome and charismatic', but we must also remember that he was an ego-driven extreme narcissist; a torturing coward who preyed on innocent young women, and he was a man – if we can call him such – who would have been scared to death if some guy had fronted him with the threat of spoiling his good looks by knocking out his teeth.

Oh, and, talking about Bundy's gnashers, I have actually handled them. The original dental casts of them, that is. These casts taken after his arrest were a huge piece of evidence in the case against him at trial. The reader may ask, 'Hey, Chris, why did Ted allow his dental casts be taken when he could have legally refused?' Could it be that a struggling Bundy was held down and his teeth impressions taken? The truth is, as prosecutor Larry Simpson told me, that

Ted was conned into giving his teeth impressions on the pretence that, as he was now in the custody of the Florida criminal justice system, he might need to see a dentist at sometime for a regular check-up so-to-speak. Being the bigoted showman that undoubtedly he was, loving the media's cameras always upon him, he wanted to look his best at all times and pearly white teeth appealed to him. What a cunning plan! What a sap!

If one lives in Eastern Europe, then the Russian serial killer Andrei Romanovich Chikatilo aka 'The Butcher of Rostov' aka 'The Red Ripper' (1936–1994) is pretty much top of the homicide pops. He raped, murdered, and mutilated at least fifty-three women and children between 1978 and 1990.

I love Russia and its people, having visited many times. I adore St Petersburg at Christmas and I love watching the 1965 movie *Dr Zhivago* starring Omar Sharif and the delectable Julie Christie. I have worked with and enjoyed the hospitality and the vodka that only Russian cops and the mafia (often both holding down the same careers at once with a nod and a wink), can offer. This seems to be quite a comfortable arrangement if you care to ask me. What could be more convenient than committing bank robberies, killing, corrupting, committing larceny, blackmailing, racketeering, running illegal girlie bars and dealing on the black market then going out and investigating the crimes yourself? Actually, neither the Russians nor the Americans invented this system of corrupt policing. Us Brits did. It started in the mid-1920s with the Liverpool City Police whose officers were so poorly paid that they became so bent they couldn't even lie straight in the own beds. At night they committed burglaries, going out to investigate them the next day. What a wheeze!

I *was* made an honoury colonel at one of the Russian Spetsnaz camps hidden deep in the forest near Buzuluk, Orenburgskaya Oblast, by hard-drinking officers at a dinner held in my honour, knowing that I am a former HM Royal Marine 'Green Beret' Commando. I also visited and filmed inside the Russian Prison for Woman at Sablino – all well documented in another of my books. During my time in Russia I learned that when the death penalty was enacted, the condemned were never given an execution time and date. When Chikatilo was taken from his cell in the Novocherkassk Prison for execution, he thought that he was being taken down the steel stairs for his weekly shower. This room is where the guards wash their dogs. There is a broken window letting in the minus thirty-degree winds. The floor is gray stone-slab with a drain in the centre. The walls are damp. There is one bare, very dim light bulb. On Monday, 14 February 1994, Chikatilo walked into this same room, an officer waited behind the door and fired a single gunshot into the monster's head. The bullet went behind his left ear to blast away part of his skull. He never felt a thing as he crumpled to the floor. Blood and brain matter were rinsed away down the drain like the mess the guard dogs make. I know all of this because I *have* visited this room. You never see the guards' faces in places like this. They wear all-black head to toe and balaclavas, and they don't take any shit either. In the UK, prison officers either in the public or private sector, are obliged to call our

British serial killers, 'Sir'. Now get your head around that if it pleases you. I think it's another damned cheek, dare I say so!

In exploring the world of the worst serial killers, it's a matter of horses for courses. All of us who have an avid interest in serial homicide will have our favourite (strike) most heinous serial murderers. Some mentally unhinged observers call killers such as Bundy 'icons'. These pathetic efforts to raise these murdering lowlives to people to be regarded as a representative symbol of something are snubbing their noses at the anguish of their victims' next-of-kin.

Perhaps another issue worth mentioning as we inexorably move toward the first chapter, is one of the killers' victimology – their preferred victim types. It's a hard fact that murder cases involving vulnerable groups like sex workers garner much less media attention than the murders of other women or the murders of children. There are exceptions, of course there are, but a man who murders innocent kiddies, as was the case with Ian Brady working in tandem with Myra Hindley, strikes to the very core of our hearts and souls.

When we explore the world of child killers, we have a horrifying number of examples. Although not serial killers, we can refer to Robert Thompson and Jon Venables, both aged ten, who abducted, tortured and killed two-year-old James Patrick Bulger on Friday, 12 February 1993. Then there is Russell Bishop, aged twenty, aka the 'Babes in the Wood' murderer of Nicola Fellows and Karan Hadaway, both aged nine, in the Wild Park, Moulsecoomb, Brighton, on 9 October 1986.

Susan Blatchford, aged eleven, and Gary Hanlon, aged twelve, were murdered by Ronald Jebson. Their bodies were found in a thicket of trees on Lippitts Hill, Epping Forest, after they went missing from their homes in Enfield, north London, on 31 March 1970. Jebson also confessed to the murder of Rosemary Papper, whom he raped and killed on 9 May 2000. Indeed, the list of heinous child killers could run to several books alone.

In Britain we have our own canon of murderers. There's 'Jack the Ripper', Colin Ireland, Steve Wright aka 'The Suffolk Strangler', Dennis Nilsen, Archibald Hall aka the 'Killer Butler', Mary Ann Cotton, Peter Bryan, Anthony Hardy aka 'The Camden Ripper', Stephen Port aka 'The Grindr Killer', Joanna Dennehy, John Duffy and David Mulcahy, Kenneth Erskine aka 'The Stockwell Strangler', Stephen Grieveson aka 'The Sunderland Strangler', Robert Maudsley aka Britain's own 'Hannibal the Cannibal', Allan Grimson, Trevor Hardy aka 'The Beast of Manchester', Michael Lupo aka 'The Wolf Man', Robert Napper, John Straffen and Peter Moore. Now can one imagine how many were, or are, across the world today, for this is just the tip of the iceberg, or should I say the caldera at the top of a soon to explode volcano.

So, it all comes down to my judgement as to who qualifies to be amongst the top ten most evil serial killers on earth. We will look at ten murderers. We will look inside their heads and examine their psychopathologies, comparing like with like. And we will be comparing them with other serial killers who could be the runners-up in this hellish contest.

So as we start, I am thinking of Chris Rea's song *The Road to Hell*, because this *is* the road *we* are about to take – RIGHT NOW!

Christopher Berry-Dee
www.christopherberrydee.com
Southsea UK & El Nido, Palawan, Philippines

Peter Kürten

'I have no remorse. As to whether recollection of my deeds
makes me feel ashamed, I will tell you. Thinking back to
all the details is not unpleasant at all. I rather enjoy it.'

Peter Kürten (1883–1931)

In deciding which serial killers found their way into
this book, I thought it would be instructive to consider
the degree of inhuman physical pain and emotional
suffering they caused to their victims before they died.
The act of killing someone is awful enough but it's the
method and the level of pain caused that leads us into
the realms of depravity.

If I can put it another way and look at capital
punishment – or 'judicial murder' as campaigners for
its abolition would call it. Stoning, or lapidation, is a
method of capital punishment where a group of people
throw rocks and stones at the condemned until the
individual dies from blunt force trauma. A particularly
barbaric example can be found on an internet video,
for on 4 November 1995 a nineteen-year-old woman
accused of adultery by the Taliban was stoned to death

in Afghanistan. Stoning is legal and practised in at least 15 other countries today, and there are fears that instances when the punishment is enacted are on the rise, particularly in Pakistan and Iraq. In many cases, the victim is also set ablaze; so while being smashed with stones, they suffer untold agony. If that is not an act of extreme depravity, I know not what is.

If we compare that with judicial hanging we might find the former British – now the US – system called 'The Long Drop' efficient and, to all intents and purposes, painless *if* carried out as intended. There are exceptions as was the case with Ali Hassan al-Majid, better known to us as 'Chemical Ali', who was hanged for his crimes against the Kurds during the 1990-91 Gulf War. He enjoyed 'The Long Drop' – so long was it that the jolt ripped his head off. Although the fatal outcome was the same whether he lost his head or not, it would have been a lot more painless than being stoned to death methinks.

Hanging in the Middle East, specifically in Iran, is carried out either by using the short drop, or being hoisted high in the air by a crane, with the person strangling over a period of several leg-kicking minutes. All gruesome and barbaric stuff, I am sure that you will agree. If a crane is not available, those who are soon-to-meet-their-maker are thrown off the top of very high buildings with the end result being terminal in every sense of the word.

It goes without saying that a condemned person suffers a great deal of anxiety whichever way they are put to death but wouldn't you agree that the quicker and more painless the execution, the easier it would be? You might even say that devils like Andrei Chikatilo got off lightly because he thought he was about to take his weekly shower then 'pop' a bullet from behind was fired and he dropped down stone dead! And we can apply similar criteria to the way serial killers treat their victims. So step forward Peter Kürten, who provides us with a terrifying yardstick by which we can judge all others of his murderous ilk.

Where do we start with Kürten? Perhaps the best word to kick off with is 'depraved'. But there are more words for Kürten: cruel; a master of evil genius; malevolent lecher; vice ridden; vile; noxious; a snake in the grass; loathsome; lousy and a murderous, blood-thirsty lump of inhumanity. There, that, at least, goes part way to describing this homicidal sadosexual killer of men, women and little girls. And it gets a lot worse, because we can also add to his richly embroidered murderous *curriculum vitae* the fact that he was a necrophiliac and also heavily into zoophilia – the latter having absolutely nothing to do with zoos but everything to do with a sexual fixation on bestiality. For Kürten, pretty much any creature with either two or four legs, feathered or not, was considered fair game. Amongst his victims was a swan – yes, he did kill a swan. It was asleep by the side of a lake. He crept up to it, cut its throat and drank the spurting warm blood! If that doesn't ruin your supper, what will?

Peter Kürten wins first prize for his depravity. His own psychiatrist, the eminent Dr. Karl Berg, labelled him the 'King of Sexual Perverts'. He can also be considered the first psychologically studied and interviewed serial killer of the twentieth century. Well done, Peter. But I can assure you this *is* as *good* as he gets.

In keeping with the theme of this book's title, we might ask ourselves where is Peter Kürten aka 'The Vampire of Düsseldorf' or 'The Düsseldorf Monster', right now? In Hell? Maybe yes, maybe no! What we *do* know is that he was guillotined in the grounds of the Klingelpütz Prison in Germany, at 6 a.m., Thursday, 2 July 1931. The actual location of any grave – if he ever had one – is unknown. The official record states that the body was 'lost or destroyed'. The prison was taken over by the Nazis after 1933 and became the main location for Gestapo interrogations and executions in the Rhineland. Over 1,000 people were executed there before the US forces liberated it in 1945. It has since been demolished and a memorial stone has been erected in the park where the prison once stood. There was one common area for all burials at Klingelpütz Prison, and it's the very same place where victims of forced labour were interred in a mass grave. Later, execution records stolen from the prison on 7 May 1945, were pored over by US Army Captains, Ulrich Orton and Charles Hepburn. The corpses were exhumed by local civilians and reburied in the Ludwigsluster Schlosspark. I'd put money on it that this is where what's left of Kürten is today.

Wherever Kürten is right now he does get another prize – he features in the book you are reading; something that I'm sure would bring this beast much postmortem glee. If you are abed as you read this, before you switch off the light make sure your bedroom door is firmly shut for this hellish Devil's spawn could be watching you right now from beyond the grave. Yes, Kürten was beheaded, and they should have driven a stake through his heart, buried him, dug him up a month later and rammed another stake through him just to make sure that he was fucking dead. Trust me, it's going to get a lot worse as we explore what made this monster.

The nature versus nurture debate, in a nutshell, explores whether human behaviour is determined by the environment, either prenatal or during an individual's life, or by his personal genes. Nature is the pre-wiring of the brain and is influenced by genetic inheritance and other biological factors. Nurture is the influence of external factors after conception: the product of exposure, experience and education on that person. It is a fascinating subject, and never more so than when criminologists try to understand the psychopathology of serial killers and mass murderers – in other words, what *made* them do what they do. Recently the debate around this has heated up considerably. It's now thought that a combination of both influences – nature *and* nurture – ultimately create the person being studied.

To give one example, I look back to the now-executed Connecticut serial killer Michael Bruce Ross (1959–2005). I interviewed Michael several times while he was on Death Row in Somers Prison and a detailed chapter exploring his life and crimes can be found in my book *Talking with Serial Killers*. He had several siblings, all of whom went through the same emotional and physical abuse at the hands of their mother as Mike had done yet he turned out to be the only rotten apple in a basket of otherwise perfectly fine fruit. This raises the question of why was it that Michael Ross turned into a sexual predator and monster while the other children didn't... Was there an evil genetic seed in play? I think not.

The case of Peter Kürten is perhaps the finest example of the interplay of nature and nurture to be found in the grim annals of criminal history. In Kürten, we find a sado-sexual, opportunist killer with a morbid love of blood, furthermore, there is a reason he became known as a vampire. He was a predator who committed a series of horrific murders and sexual assaults in and around the city of Düsseldorf, with his victimology and MO varying over time. So let's try and conduct a granular examination of his psychopathology, as best as we can.

A Gemini, Kürten was born on Sunday, 26 May 1883, at Mülheim am Rhein across the river from Stadtkreis Köln (Cologne) in what is now the state of Nordrhein-Westfalen, Germany. He was born to a dirt-poor family, and he was one of no less than thirteen children, two of whom died at an early age. To further put this into perspective they all lived in a cluttered one-bedroomed apartment. Various sources cite him as being the third sibling, elsewhere he is the fifth child and others claim he was the eldest.

The matriarch was occasionally with the drink to drown her sorrows because her husband – a sand-caster (moulder) in a timber factory by trade – was a brutal alcoholic. Herr Kürten, when in his cups, often forced his wife and children into a room before ordering his pitiful spouse to strip naked and raping her as the kids looked on. So we can be sure that Frau Kürten suffered from extreme physical and psychological abuse throughout her married life, as did the children from the moment they were born into this particularly disgusting home environment. Indeed, Frau Kürten was so miserable that she eventually begged her husband to kill her and end it all. However, she must have had a change of heart because she didn't want to leave her kids behind. All of this suited Herr Kürten for he had no intention of bringing any release to his wife let alone bringing thirteen children up on his own.

Despite his dysfunctional formative years, young Peter was a good scholar. But why was he a good student when his home life was such a car wreck? I think that the answer rests with the fact that school provided him with a stable, structured environment. He could take his tutors' discipline on the chin, so he flourished academically. But, unlike his siblings, something wicked had started to metamorphose within his mind. He became a killer at the age of nine, no less.

In the testimony Kürten later gave to his psychiatrist, Dr. Berg, he claimed that he had murdered two of his playmates while rafting on the River Rhine. He had pushed one lad into the water knowing that he couldn't swim and, when the other boy attempted to save him, Kürten pushed that lad's head under the water too. One might suggest that he made all of this up, but he had a remarkable memory for the details of all of his heinous crimes. Even many years later and under the most severe interrogation he was never exposed telling untruths or gilding the lily. There can be no doubt that two of his playmates *did* drown in the river. At the time he'd denied foul play, telling the police who recovered the bodies that it had been an accident. With no other witnesses, the deaths were deemed accidental. Those that have read Dennis Wheatley's 1953 novel *To the Devil a Daughter* may be thinking that, in Kürten, we have *To the Devil a Son*.

By chance, one of the lodgers in the same building as the Kürten family was the local authority's dogcatcher. A more correct name for this occupation during this period in Germany was actually 'dog killer' and for this kind of sadistic work a sadistic nature was, quite obviously, an employment requirement. Moreover, it was this dog killer who taught young Kürten how to torture the animals he caught.

So here we have a young lad being brought up in a shocking home environment ruled by a lumpen beast of a father and with his mother at her wits' end. By the age of nine he becomes a killer, more than able to tell bald-faced lies to the police and being educated in sadism and the abuse of terrified, helpless animals. Certainly not the best start in life, of this we might all agree upon. To escape his father's mistreatment, young Kürten often ran away from home; sometimes he was away for days, even weeks on end.

FBI offender profiler, John Douglas, says that Kürten's overall early behaviour exhibited all the signs of a serial killer in the making. He 'reacted to a chronically abusive upbringing when he engaged in violence towards animals and set fires. He abused animals because it gave him control, something he did not have as a victim of his father's beatings.' Speaking of Kürten's penchant for arson, Douglas adds, 'He set fires because it also gave him a sense of control over other people.' John Douglas's observation can rightly be applied to a number of other serial killers, and we can include Henry Lee Lucas, Ottis Toole and Arthur Shawcross amongst them. As many of my readers know, I interviewed both Henry Lucas and Arthur Shawcross aka 'The Monster of the Rivers'.

The latter, as a youngster pulled the feathers out of live birds and put kittens in sacks only to throw them into a pond to watch the helpless creatures drown. Their early behaviour mirrors that of Kürten. This is not true of all serial killers though, there is no evidence whatsoever that Ted Bundy, for example, was ever cruel to animals or that he was an arsonist although he did enjoy stealing. I also interviewed Douglas Daniel Clark aka 'The Sunset Slayer', and 'Doug' loved cats and dogs, like Bundy.

In 1896, thirteen-year-old Peter Kürten met a girl of his own age. Somewhat echoing his mentally imprinted experiences of watching his mother being forced to undress and be violently raped by her husband, he asked this young girl to undress and have sex with him. Given this, we might assume that he found the domestic violence he witnessed quasi-erotic. The girl – probably responding to some form of threat or coercion – initially complied but she denied him sex. This would have infuriated young Kürten for it had to be obvious to him then that he had failed to live up to his father's own overpowering control over his wife. Peter, therefore, tried something else to get satisfaction: he resorted to committing bestiality with sheep, pigs and goats to achieve ejaculation. Years later, after his arrest for serial murder, Kürten told his psychiatrist that he could only achieve an orgasm with these animals by stabbing and slashing them to death with increasing ferocity.

This may seem as if I am stating the obvious, but serial killers do not simply pop up out of the blue. There is a 'graduation period' as they progress from minor sex offences such as stalking, to committing sexual assaults on to rape, serial rape, then they finally cross the threshold into murder before fully emerging as a sexual serial killer. They go through a learning process. They develop what are called 'murder kits'. They experiment and find the tools that suit them best for their homicidal purposes: rope; plastic sheeting to avoid soiling the interiors of their vehicles; handcuffs – indeed, whatever instruments best suit them for the entrapping and killing of their victims. During this graduation period a need to increase the pleasure he receives from each event develops. He becomes addicted to the sexual adrenalin rush which increases prior to the kill and culminates in the murder itself. After this, the 'high' rapidly disappears until his cravings start all over again. Each 'event' then increases in ferocity as the need to satisfy himself grows. And, of course, with each kill, he grows in confidence. Often this ultimately proves to be his undoing and leads to capture by law enforcement. His very psychopathology tells him that he is smarter than the law but of course he cannot be!

Already a double killer at such a young age, Peter Kürten is a textbook example of this perverted sexual metamorphosing. Committing bestiality was, for him, a mere stepping stone towards committing rape, serial rape and then multiple sadistic homicides. Added to the psychological mix that was Peter Kürten, we also have compulsive masturbation; compulsive sexual behaviour; hyperphilia; problematic hypersexuality; sexual addiction; sexual compulsivity; sexual dependency; out-of-control sexual antisocial behaviour and paraphilia. In young Kürten, we pretty much have a fully blown homicidal psychopath in the making who is bound to wreak havoc on society in the very near future. This is a blood-chilling scenario. Indeed, when we delve deep into the minds of most sexually motivated serial murderers – John Reginald Christie, Michael Ross, Henry Lee Lucas, John Wayne Gacy, Ted Bundy, Kenneth Bianchi, Harvey Carignan, Arthur Shawcross, Peter Sutcliffe – we will find similar back-narratives running through them like threads of steel wire.

In 1897, Kürten was fourteen years old and had finished school. He continued to run away from home repeatedly until his brutal father, sick and tired of this, got him a woodwork apprenticeship at his own place of work. After a year, Kürten repaid his father by breaking into the premises and stealing around 300 marks (roughly equivalent to £3,600 or US$7,700 in today's money) a not inconsiderable sum in those austere, impoverished times. Four days after the burglary, he was arrested and sent to a juvenile detention centre where he spent one month in custody. In November 1899 – according to Kürten's 1930 confessions – he strangled a young woman while they were having sex in a wood and left her for dead. As no body was ever found, and no complaint against Kürten was ever made, it is to be presumed that she survived and for whatever reason she chose to say nothing about her near-death experience.

But now it was time for Herr Kürten Sr. to get his just desserts and, ironically, it was his son's burglary that served it up on a plate. During the course of the investigation into the theft, police interviewed Frau Kürten and her children and, in doing so, the cops learned that the patriarch had been forcing himself on his thirteen-year-old daughter. Kürten senior was arrested and sent to prison for three years. This was the break Frau Kürten had been praying for. She obtained a separation order, relocated to Düsseldorf and, three years later, remarried before disappearing into obscurity and history.

> 'I got pleasure from the glow of the fire, the cries for help. It gave me so much pleasure that I got sexual satisfaction.'
>
> *Peter Kürten: to his psychiatrist*

After his short stint at the reform school, Kürten continued his career in crime, and added arson to his repertoire. He set ablaze haylofts and barns, thrilled as everything went up in flames and smoke, and hoping that a tramp may have been sleeping in the hay. An extremely angry young man, he attempted eight strangulations, carried out two axe attacks as well as the numerous acts of arson. He was in prison for a large part of two decades, the longest stretch lasting from 1905 until 1913. And German society wouldn't have to wait too long after his release before he struck again, and he did so with a ferocity that is more terrifying than any inventive horror screenplay writer could come up with.

Peter Klein was a savvy businessman and the owner of the 'Wirtshaus Peter Klein Schenke' a three-storey tavern on a corner of a busy Mülheim an der Ruhr intersection, making it a popular place to drink and stay. Klein had a ten-year-old daughter called Christine.

Kürten had been robbing places for months and as a customer he knew *vermieter*, Peter Klein. This, however, did not deter him from deciding to rob the man. So, during the night of Sunday, 25 May 1913, he broke into the tavern, intending to take as much jewellery and cash as he could lay his hands on. The Kleins were asleep and he crept around the premises until he suddenly spied the little girl in her bed. She was wearing pyjamas and tucked up under thick covers. Almost instantly the thought of robbing the place vanished and he became overwhelmed and possessed by the idea of raping and killing the girl. For a few seconds, Christine might have thought that she was having a nightmare. After his arrest, Kürten recalled that she woke up and struggled for some time as he strangled her with his bare hands while rocking her head backwards and forwards. He then slit her throat from ear to ear. The sight of the gaping wound, the vivid red colour of her blood and the gurgling noise the wound made, sent him into a sexual frenzy. He began cuddling the dying child while masturbating until he ejaculated. Kürten then quietly left. What follows is Kürten's recollection of the murder of Christine Klein to police and it makes for sickening reading:

'I broke into the house in the Wolfstrasse – an inn owned by Klein ... I went up to the first floor. I opened different doors and found nothing worth stealing; but in the bed I saw a sleeping girl of about ten covered by a thick feather bedspread ... I drew her head over the edge of the bed and penetrated her [genitals] with my fingers.

I had a small but sharp pocket-knife with me and I held the child's head and cut her throat. I heard the blood spurt and drip on the mat beside the bed. It spurted in an arch, right over my hand. The whole thing lasted about three minutes. Then I went, locked the door and went back home to Düsseldorf.'

It is worth pausing here, so we can try to begin to imagine the sheer terror this sweet little girl went through as she realised that this was to be a real nightmare, one from which she would never wake. The following day Kürten returned and sat drinking beer in a café directly opposite the Wirtshaus, gloating at all of the police activity going on around him. This was a practice he would later repeat time and again. Returning to the scene of the crime is a perverse behaviour acted out by many other serial killers too.

If anything *could* have put Kürten back on track it might have been military service. But the very thought of redeeming a fully emerged sexual psychopath is simply pie in the sky because psychopaths can *never* be cured. Nevertheless, in 1914 war had broken out, and thirty-one-year-old Kürten was conscripted into the Kaiser's Imperial Army (*Deutsches Heer*). He soon deserted, was subsequently caught and sent to a military prison where he became so troublesome that he spent most of his time in solitary confinement. He was freed in 1921. Now aged thirty-eight he married a sweet shop owner and former sex worker, Auguste Scharf. Scharf had been jailed for four years for shooting a man who jilted her after promising marriage. She had since repented for her sins and was now a changed woman who would go on to stick by Kürten through thick and thin. She seemed to be totally unaware that she was sleeping with one of the most evil of *all* serial killers in world history.

On Sunday, 3 February 1929, while tramping through a snowy Düsseldorf during his lunch break Kürten spotted elderly woman, Frau Maria Kuhn. He followed her for a short distance and felt an erection forming in his trousers. Swiftly he grabbed her by the lapels and pulled the frail lady into some bushes. In all, he stabbed her with scissors at least twenty-four times but she managed to survive because although many of the stabs he inflicted went so deep that they impacted bone, they were slowed down by her heavy coat. He later confessed: 'the place where I attacked Frau Kuhn, I visited that same evening twice and later several times. In doing so, I sometimes had an orgasm.'

This might seem a totally unprofessional thing for a criminologist to suggest, but do we not see hallmarks of demonic possession here in Herr Kürten? Many of us have seen the 1973 horror movie *The Exorcist*, which was inspired by real-life events. Played by Linda Blair, the possessed ten-year-old child, Regan, goes from a sweet kid one moment to evil personified the next, and reverts back and forth time and again. Whether or not you believe in this spooky stuff is up to you, but there are many well-documented examples to be found on the internet if you want to be scared witless, or shitless, that is. My point is that there can be *no doubt* that Peter Kürten *was* possessed by *something* disgustingly malevolent, and that evil perhaps lay dormant in his mind for much of the time. In those periods he seemed to be a perfectly normal, innocuous looking man who would not have hurt a fly – then he would suddenly become overwhelmed by the beast that was sleeping within. Can we perhaps see the analogy here between Regan and Kürten... or am I asking too much of the reader to even consider this? I think not, and I am about to explain why.

On Saturday, 9 February (just six days after the attack on Frau Kuhn) Peter Kürten happened across eight-year-old Rosa Ohliger as she played near her home. He waited for a chance to pounce, which came when she strayed a little too far. He grabbed the girl from behind, cupping her mouth and trying to choke her unconscious. Carrying the struggling child fifty yards into a nearby heavily wooded area he took out his scissors and stabbed Rosa three times in the neck and heart, killing her almost instantly. Despite already having had an orgasm, he was once again possessed with the urge to have sex with the dead body, but something made him stop. He had an animal sense he was being watched. He panicked. He didn't want to get caught so he moved Rosa's body a little further away and pushed her under a hedge. He then, according to his own account, went to the cinema before going home. Early the next morning he crept out of his bed and picked up a bottle of petrol. Risking the hue and cry being raised about the missing child, he returned to the child's body, doused her in the fluid and set her alight, hoping to burn away any evidence connecting him to the murder. As Rosa's body started to burn the smell of the sizzling flesh gave him another erection. Then he made a run for it using trees as cover and was back at his home in minutes.

'When that morning I poured petrol over the child, Ohliger, and set fire to her, I had an orgasm at the height of the fire.'

Peter Kürten's testimony to police
on the murder of Rosa Ohliger

Later that very same morning Kürten returned to the area again. Drinking Altbier in a nearby tavern, he watched the public and police commotion unfold. He even had the nerve to talk to a police officer for twenty minutes about what had occurred. This habit of returning to crime scenes and ingratiating oneself with police is a familiar one amongst the serial killer ilk. It is, in my opinion, another form of mental masturbation; the gloating of the psychopathological mindset of individuals who believe they can outwit the police. They are in control. It is a way of mocking the police who simply have no clue that the killer they are looking for is secretly laughing, not behind their backs but straight into their faces. This is something Arthur Shawcross did on several occasions. Also Kenneth Bianchi, one of the two notorious Los Angeles 'Hillside Stranglers' who went for rides in police cars on pretence of joining the LAPD, all while the strangler was being hunted and the entire city of LA reduced to a state of panic. I have interviewed both. I also interviewed Texas's most notorious serial killer, the now-executed Kenneth Allen McDuff (1946–1998). McDuff even applied for a job as a law enforcement officer while he was out and about killing – and that takes some brass balls, if I say so myself!

Rosa's body was badly burned, but an autopsy determined that her killer had stabbed her in the stomach, temple and genitalia, ejaculating and spilling his semen – his 'Devil's Seed' – over her knickers and inserting it into her vagina with his smeared fingers. Without even attempting to go ballistic with hyperbole, if that wasn't the work of a demon, I don't know what is. Demons come from Hell, do they not?

Kürten's MO changed on Thursday, 14 February 1929. The now blue-collar Flingern-Nord suburb of Düsseldorf became the location for the next murder when the body of a forty-five-year-old Rudolf Scheer was found lying by the side of a road. Scheer was a well-respected mechanic. He had been stabbed to death. Once again Kürten brazenly revisited the crime scene and started talking with police, telling them, 'I hope you catch the bastard soon.' Whatever the case, the motive for this killing remains unknown. It is highly likely that, having not found a female victim that day, with his overwhelming sexual needs unmet, the very act of stabbing and the spurting of blood were sufficient enough. Between February and August 1929, the record shows that Peter Kürten took a relative break from his killing – only half-strangling four women who all survived. I somewhat doubt that he had intended to 'half strangle' these females. Murder was his intent, and these four victims had lucky escapes for one reason or another. But Kürten hadn't really started yet. Indeed, he wasn't even off the starting blocks.

The various accounts for the Sunday, 11 August 1929 strangulation and stabbing homicide of pretty Maria Hahn contain a mixed bag of errors. Some writers erroneously say she was eleven years old but the truth is that she was twenty and worked as a domestic servant. According to Kürten, and he is not to be disbelieved, he first came across her sitting on a street bench, on Thursday, 8 August, and he described her as 'a girl looking for marriage'. They chatted briefly, but before parting company, they arranged to meet on the 11th. Once again, the literature on Kürten is confusing at best. One published source has her murdered on Thursday, 29 August, while another true crime writer is even more vague throwing in either August 14 or 15 as the date of the murder. The killer himself was absolutely clear that he killed Maria Hahn on the 11th – and Sundays were often, by tradition, a domestic servant's day off.

The murder weapon in the Hahn case is yet another matter of uncertainty, with some claiming it was a knife, others that it was scissors. The confusion is unsurprising considering that her body was not found for three months. Forensic evidence, however, shows that the stabs administered to her throat, breasts and head were inflicted with scissors – and this was supported by Kürten's testimony.

Kürten's recollections of every detail of his gruesome murders, the dates, times and places were always spot-on. Like an overzealous homicidal accountant he was fastidious about the details, although he occasionally came up with two different versions of the same event.

Maria Hahn's rendezvous with 'The German Grim Reaper' (*Der Deutsche Grimmig Sensenmann*) began with the two of them spending a couple of hours together that sunny Sunday. Then Kürten lured this young woman – whom he now described as 'a loose-living domestic servant who was willing to offer me quite a lot' – into a meadow so that he could rape and kill her. According to this vile man, she repeatedly pleaded with him to spare her life as he alternately strangled her, stabbed her in the chest and head and sat astride her waiting for her to die. He later buried Maria's body in a cornfield, only to return to her corpse many times to masturbate

– behaviour similar to that of the Connecticut serial killer, Michael Bruce Ross, who returned to several of his victims, including two little schoolgirls. Kürten had the additional sickening intention of nailing Maria's rotting remains to a tree in a mock crucifixion to shock and disgust the public. Once again, this type of revolting behaviour is not as unusual as it first seems. Kenneth Bianchi and his half-cousin, Angelo Buono aka 'The Hillside Stranglers' did much the same thing by dumping the naked bodies (some with their legs spread-eagled) of their victims alongside roads, at a garbage dump site and one partly thrown over a canyon's edge. The monsters' intention was to shock to death anyone who happened upon them. In the UK, Joanna Dennehy, the thirty-three-year-old British serial killer, dumped the almost naked corpses of three men in water-filled ditches near Peterborough. One victim, a married man called Kevin Lee who had two adoring children, was wearing a black, sequined dress which was pulled up over his buttocks. An aerosol can was inserted into his anus, there for the world to see. My definitive account of the Dennehy murders is *Love of Blood* and was written with the full cooperation of police if you want to know more about this case. In the case of Maria Hahn, according to Kürten, her body was too heavy to lift. Besides it was, by now, quite literally falling to pieces and the stench must have been almost unbearable. So instead of creating his macabre crucifixion scene, he returned to the shallow grave to embrace and caress her as he lay underneath the cadaver. Well, you wouldn't wish to come upon such a terrible scene of necrophilia on a deathly quiet moonlit night, would *you*? Fuck that!

During the early morning of Wednesday, 21 August, Kürten randomly stabbed an eighteen-year-old girl, a thirty-year-old man, and a thirty-seven-year-old woman in separate attacks. All three were seriously wounded, and they told police their assailant had not spoken a word before he went for them. Then, on Saturday, 24 August, with his lust for blood still unquenched, Kürten noticed five-year-old Gertrude Hamacher and her foster sister Luise Lenzen, aged fourteen.

It was the time of the annual fair along the banks of the River Rhine. Ever the predator, Kürten was prowling through the bustling crowds hunting for a victim when he zeroed in on Gertrude and Luise as they were walking home through the relatively quiet Flehe district of Düsseldorf. It was about 10.30 p.m., so not really an appropriate time of night for parents to allow their little kids to wander around in the dark. Furthermore, the girls were using unlit back alleys to avoid the still busy streets and so were unwittingly walking into a death trap from which escape would prove impossible.

Then he swooped.

Kürten appeared, as if from nowhere, in front of the girls and politely asked Luise to run an errand for him. 'Would you please go and buy some cigarettes for me?' he asked pointing towards the fair. Although Luise was slightly taken aback, she had been raised to do as her elders told her, so she took some money from Kürten and ran off to find cigarettes. As soon as Luise was out of sight, Kürten picked Gertrude up in his arms then walked out of the alleyway over to bushes bordering an allotment. Here, in a patch of runner beans, he began strangling her with such force he later said he felt as though her eyes might pop from her skull. He then pulled a knife out of his pocket and slit her throat, killing her almost instantly.

Luise had run quickly back to the alley, stopping short when she saw the stranger was alone and that Gertrude was gone. 'Did you get my cigarettes?' Kürten asked, smiling. She handed the pack to him and, in a flash, he grabbed her wrists. Within moments she had been dragged, struggling, to where the body of Gertrude now lay dead and covered with blood. Giggling, Kürten choked the young girl and fondled her breasts and vagina. Finally, after having an orgasm, he used his knife to slice her throat from ear-to-ear.

Kürten later described how he had watched the blood seep from Gertrude's neck. First, he touched it with his fingers and rubbed his fingers together, staring at it. Later, at trial, he explained to a horrified court how Luise's blood felt. He told them the colour made him 'happy again because I wanted to know what it tasted like'. It was alleged by police that he also bit Luise around the knife wound in the left side of her neck indicating that he was either trying to eat her skin or suck her blood like a vampire. Kürten admitted several times to sucking blood from the necks of his victims – one of which being the swan he'd killed. Both girls were now dead and Kürten lay on the ground masturbating over them for some time before calmly folding his knife and strolling away without a care in the world.

The following day Gertrude and Luise's bodies were found, but his bloodthirsty demonic urges rose again. He strangled and drowned a girl only known as 'Anni', and tried the same with Christine Heerstrausse; then went on to stab Anna Goldhausen, Frau Mantel and Gustav Kornblum.

At this point in the narrative, the reader might be thinking of Kürten as being insane: nuts; stark raving bonkers; a prime candidate for Bedlam and as mad as the proverbial 'hatter' or even 'the March Hare'. But But let's look at the legal definition of 'insanity' because so many headline grabbers label these monsters we call serial killers as 'madmen', when they are not.

The M'Naghten Rules date from 1843 when a Daniel M'Naghten attempted to murder the then Prime Minister, Sir Robert 'Bobby' Peel (1788–1850) also the father of modern British policing, owing to his founding of the Metropolitan Police Service – and the reason we've called police officers, amongst other names, 'Bobbies' or 'Peelers', here in the UK. Across the pond some cops should be called 'Redneck Murdering Scumbags' including the killers of forty-six-year-old George Floyd – Minneapolis cops Derek Chauvin; Tou Thao; Thomas Lane and J. Alexander Kueng. Their actions on Monday, 25 May 2020 gave rise to the 'Black Lives Matter' movement that now justifiably resonates around the world and will do so for decades to come.

Moving swiftly on, it was clear to doctors that M'Naghten was not the full wicket – he was mentally unstable or a few sandwiches short of a picnic as some might say. But what the jury had to decide was whether he was so unhinged that he did not know the difference between right and wrong. If he was, Lord Chief Justice Tindal told the jury, then he could not be held responsible for his actions. Indeed, this was the conclusion the jury reached and the public outcry that greeted M'Naghten's release led to the formation of the 'M'Naghten Rules'. 'In order to establish a defence on the grounds of insanity, it must be clearly proved that, at the time of the committing of the act, the party accused was labouring under such a defect of reason, from disease of the mind as to not know the nature and quality of the act.'

One might think that forensic psychiatry would have an easy ride in deciding *precisely* what madness is with regard to the serial killing behaviour of psychopaths like Kürten, but – oh Lordy – it doesn't quite work out this way. Many defence lawyers will argue that their client was only overtaken by madness at the moment when the crime was committed – otherwise he behaves like any other sane human being. Temporary criminal insanity some call it and I don't buy into at all – it's hogwash.

Dr. Ronald Markham, an American forensic psychiatrist who gave evidence in the trials of Charles Manson and the aforementioned 'Hillside Stranglers', believed that it remains 'beyond the scope of medicine to decide whether criminal insanity may be only temporary.' He added, 'One problem is there is no objective method for evaluating one psychiatrist's view of whether a defendant is insane and dangerous against a conflicting opinion.' Another problem Dr. Markham identifies is the guile used by many insane criminals in imitating behaviour that seems rational. But there are also cases in the US of inmates who have returned to sanity but are kept in an asylum because a psychiatrist is afraid of being sued if he recommends their release and his judgement proves wrong. Dr. Markham writes that few psychiatrists 'can give a medically accurate evaluation time after time.'

What a remarkably tactful man Dr. Markham is. I am most certainly not when it comes to this as it is fact that criminal case histories are littered with forensic psychiatrists who haven't a clue as to what planet they are living on. I'm aware that I can be accused of self-promotion here – but to quote from the cover of *Talking with Psychopaths and Savages: A journey into the evil mind*, one of my other international bestsellers: '… the author had the chance to interview his subjects' psychiatrists and, in doing so, uncovered a terrible truth: a monster can be hidden behind a friendly face. Some of these experts proved to have more in common with their patients than one would ever have expected.'

So could it be seriously suggested that Kürten was only *temporarily* insane when he committed his dreadful crimes? The simple answer is no. We can apply the same diagnostic criteria to just about every other serial killer past, present and into the future, because you see this temporary insanity malarkey is most always a defence mitigation… a sort of excuse to try and lessen the penalty for the crimes. So, if the reader ever hears a defence lawyer rattle out that old, well-worn, well-trodden 'temporary insanity' rubbish, substitute it in your mind with 'utter bullshit'. The tactic rarely works anyway. And, just for the fun of it, here is one of my invented scenarios. Trust me when I say this sort of stuff goes on every day in courtrooms throughout the US of

A with Mr Attorney waving his arms around and smiling sympathetically to the jury:

'Ya'll hear now, ya good folk when I tell ya'll that Willie Bean here is accused of multiple murders. An' guess what folks? He says he done 'em all. Yes, folks he dun raped an' he dun kilt twenty-six of your neighbourly young gals. An' as God is *my* witness, Willie is a hard-working man. Married for fourteen years, being a loving husband to several former wives and some others and he's raised quite a few kids I can tell ya'll this much (cheeky nod and a wink). And guess what else? He's got a degree in the social sciences and some certificates from his other profession (rap sheets). But he dun never kilt anyone until he was overtaken by what we call, "them sudden bouts of temporary insanity". (Reaching for a Holy Bible and holding it aloft) Willie is a churchgoer. He loves Our Lord. An' ya'll hear that immediately prior to each of his killings he was nice and neighbourly... had just finished studying for a Doctorate Degree. Then an hour later he raped and bludgeoned Miss Phillips to death with a tyre iron, dug a shallow grave, changed the number plates on his veehickle an' he just dun drove home and cleaned up his yard, burned his clothes and shoes, an' then he, um, read the Bible to his wife in bed. Ummm an' then tried to pop another bun in the oven.

'Ya'll see, members of the jury, our Willie here is just the same as you and me. Country folk... with real homemade apple-pie family values... a normal guy who was for some ~~fucking~~ (stenographer's deletion) reason overtaken by temporary insanity.

'I thank you. The defense rests!'

I hope you catch my drift there but now we must get serious and return to Peter Kürten.

★

Peter Kürten was not just evil, he transcended evil. He was and he still is the epitome of evil personified. He has to be amongst the foulest of serial killers ever to have walked the face of God's earth. Even though his crimes were committed over a century ago we can still grasp the enormity of how we would feel if such a monster was creeping around one of our cities today.

'Hello. You are very beautiful. My name is Fritz Baumgart.'
Peter Kürten: on meeting Gertrude Schulte

Various writers attribute various dates to the attack on Gertrude Schulte; however, I am satisfied that it actually took place on Sunday, 25 August 1929, a day after he murdered the young sisters.

Gertrude, with seductive eyes and full lips, was a raven-haired beauty to be sure. Aged twenty-seven, she made her living by helping a family with housework, doing domestic chores and looking after their children at their home near Neuss, just outside Düsseldorf. It transpires that, at about 2 p.m. on that Sunday, she finished her work and went to meet a few friends. This was a get-together that she'd never make because, on her way, Gertrude met Kürten. Initially she thought him not unattractive.

It has been said that Kürten, like so many smooth-talking sexual psychopaths, had always possessed a confidence about him that women seemingly liked. Whether this is true or not is another matter; however, he did take care of his physical appearance by eating properly, he stayed well dressed in a dapper sort of way and he kept fit. Indeed, he would not stand out in any metropolis even now being just one man amongst a million or so others – it was all part of his social camouflage, the man sitting behind you on a bus, crowded in with you on a commuter-packed train, or the 'nice man' amiably chatting to young girls in a park as dusk falls. Can you see him now? The humanoid beast inside Kürten was invisible but it was there, hiding and breathing under his skin.

For her part, Gertrude's pretty face and slim figure attracted many men. But she was also a confident, streetwise young woman and rarely took up their advances because she knew that all they wanted was her body. Therefore, Kürten's opening gambit of 'Hello. You are beautiful. My name is Fritz Baumgart,' fell on deaf ears. It was all a bit too oily for her and there was something about him that was creepy, so Gertrude politely rejected him. It may have been a shrug of her shoulders, maybe a smile accompanied with a 'thank you but no', or it could have been a two-fingered 'fuckkkk off you creep!' – I rather like the idea of the latter, don't you? Nevertheless, getting more sexually aroused by the heartbeat, he persisted with a charm offensive unlikely to knock any woman off her feet: 'Let's say we go somewhere and have sex,' he suggested bluntly. Gertrude's reply was cutting in every sense of the word: 'I'd rather die,' she said as she turned her back on him to walk away. 'Die then,' snapped the now enraged Kürten. He closed in on her and stabbed her in the back thirteen times. He let her fall to her knees and left her to die. But die, she didn't! Gertrude Schulte survived her encounter with Peter Kürten.

Despite a massive police manhunt for the as yet unidentified serial killer, there was no respite for the *volk* of Düsseldorf throughout September. In an effort to throw detectives off his scent by using a different MO, he changed his attack weapon from scissors to a hammer and sometimes used a rope to choke his victims into unconsciousness. He attacked Sofie Ruckl, according to him, with a chisel, and tried to strangle Maria Rad. Both were lucky to escape with their lives. Then Kürten bludgeoned Ida Reuter to death with a hammer. In her case, once again various accounts give conflicting details and dates. One source states that on Friday, 6 September 1929 thirteen-year-old Ida Reuter was found dead; face down and with her panties tugged off, in a field in Flehe. Unlike the previous homicides Herr Kürten had committed, this source noted that the killer 'did not strangle or stab Ida, but … he had shaken and beaten her to death with his hands and fists.' This account is a bit of a mystery as Ida Reuter was in fact a domestic worker aged thirty-one. Other sources state that she was killed on either 29 or 30 September. To avoid confusion reigning supreme, the most accurate version of events must, surely, be those from the police records, the forensic evidence and the later statement made by the killer himself.

The official report tells us that at 7 a.m. on Monday, 30 September, a woman's body was found in the meadows beside the Rhine 'lying in a posture typical of sexual outrages,' on her back, with her knickers pulled off. She had been raped – probably after death had occurred. There was also evidence that the body had been dragged a considerable distance.

What we also know from Kürten's confession was that he met the youthful-looking thirty-one-year-old at Düsseldorf railway station. He persuaded her to accompany him to a café and afterwards they went for a stroll through Der Hofgarten close to the River Rhine. As darkness fell, Ida wanted to turn back – which they did. But, once they were out of sight of other walkers, Kürten pulled a hammer out of his pocket and hit her on the right temple before dragging her unconscious body further into the dark. There, he dealt her more hammer blows about the head and raped her. Becoming aware of people relatively nearby, Kürten then dragged her body further into the fields.

Dr. Karl Berg's forensic report (published in his book *Der Sadist*, 1932) states that the injuries were consistent with: '*Wiederholte schwere hammerschlage von einem hammer mit quadratischem gesicht,*' or: 'repeated heavy hammer blows from a square-faced hammer.'

In October 1929, Elisabeth Dorrier was killed. And, once again, published accounts disagree over the details with some suggesting that she was eleven years old, while others have her age as around twenty-two. At the root of this confusion may be a photograph that purports to be of Elisabeth Dorrier. The small grey snapshot of a girl's face could depict a girl of around eleven, or it could be of a fresh-faced young woman in her twenties. Either way, the photo is undated and could have been taken years before Kürten took her life.

A number of sources state that the killing took place on Saturday, 12 October, which it might just have. Some narratives report that Kürten picked up a servant girl as she walked along the pavement about a mile from her residence and took her to nearby bushes where he suffocated her until she fell unconscious. He then, they say, stabbed her about twenty-two times until she bled out and died. Although plausible, this account directly contradicts both forensic evidence and Kürten's testimony. It's all a bit of a criminological pickle I'm afraid to say.

By now it must be remembered that the city of Düsseldorf was in turmoil, with equal amounts of panic, speculation and theorising about the 'Vampire of Düsseldorf', or sometimes the 'Düsseldorf Monster', abounding in the headline-grabbing press and in the streets and cafés. So it is understandable that contemporary accounts might be inaccurate and contradictory. However, recourse to forensic reports and the account given by Kürten himself lead me to believe that the following scenario is, by a long chalk, the most accurate I can come up with. It is worth noting that the circumstances and MO closely reflect the murder of Ida Reuter not quite a fortnight earlier.

At about 9 p.m. on Friday, 11 October 1929, Kürten put his hammer into his hip pocket and set off for a walk. He was the archetypal 'opportunist' serial killer, and as he passed by a theatre, he encountered Elisabeth Dorrier, a servant girl, and suggested they walk together, probably after ingratiating himself with his usual opener: 'You are beautiful.' She was reluctant at first but accompanied him to a bar for a drink and there he was able to dispel any suspicions she had with his smooth chat and warm smiles. Can you see them sitting together now? I can.

After the drink, her head perhaps a bit fuzzy, they took a train to Gräfenberg and went for a stroll along the Düssel – a small tributary of the River Rhine. As they walked along the path Kürten suddenly struck her once across the right temple with his hammer. She dropped to the ground instantly and he raped her, battering her about the head repeatedly with his hammer. She was found, horribly injured and unconscious at about 6.30 a.m. on Saturday, 12 October. She died the following day without regaining consciousness.

Then, on Friday, 25 October 1929, Kürten attacked two women with his hammer. Frau Meurer and Frau Wanders both survived – although in the second attack this was purely thanks to an act of God because the hammer handle broke. On Thursday, 7 November – somewhat miraculously this *is* a date agreed upon by everyone – Kürten snatched five-year-old, blue-eyed Gertrude Albermann. He had been stalking the girl for several weeks. He knew that her parents often took her to play in a Flingern district park near their home. He had also noticed that her mother often spent much time gossiping with other folk, all of which allowed the curious little girl to explore and sometimes briefly stray, though not too far away. On this day, he was hiding in bushes sexually primed and ready to pounce.

She was there... he grabbed her; cupping her mouth so she couldn't scream out. Then he calmly walked with her almost a mile to an area he had selected as his killing place. Choking her unconscious, he pulled out his knife (some erroneously say it was scissors) and stabbed Gertrude thirty-six times until she bled out. Kürten later told police that he had stared at her for some time. He went back and forth in his mind over whether he should sexually violate her or set her on fire. He chose something quite different. Picking up the child's body he carried her almost half a mile to a nearby factory, where, outside the walls, he told Dr. Berg, he stabbed her again and raped her postmortem. The autopsy results supported his account. He then made a makeshift grave for her out of rubbish and bricks and calmly walked away.

Two days after Gertrude's distraught parents had reported her as missing to police, an editor at a local newspaper received a cryptic letter, headed, 'Murder at Pappendelle'; the content of which indicated that the body could be found near a factory wall. Enclosed with the letter was a roughly drawn map marked with an 'X'. Almost immediately police believed that the writer was the girl's killer. They rushed to the scene and amongst nettles they found Gertrude's little body.

In February 1930, Kürten tried to strangle a woman known only as 'Hilda'. On Sunday, 30 March, he attempted to strangle two women known only as 'Maria' and 'Irma'. Then on Wednesday, 30 April, came the attempted throttling of Sibilla Hau, and another girl whose name is unknown, followed by an attack on Charlotte Ulrich who sustained serious injuries, and several other young women – *all* on the same day!

On Friday, 16 May, Kürten had consensual sexual relations with Gertrude Bell, whom he did not hurt. Indeed, according to her testimony he told her that she was 'too good' for him and that he was a 'bad man' – being a sublimely modest understatement if ever there was one. Nevertheless, it was events just before this encounter with Fräulein Bell that proved to be his undoing.

On Wednesday, 14 May 1930, Maria Budlick, a twenty-year-old unemployed domestic servant, had taken a train from Cologne to Düsseldorf in search of employment. At Düsseldorf Central Station she was approached by a man who offered to help her find a hostel. So began the turn of events that would soon put Kürten's neck under the guillotine's razor-sharp blade and his head dropping into a burlap sack.

The stranger was a presentable sort of chap, but Maria was skeptical. Nevertheless, she agreed to follow him; not feeling afraid, and as they walked and talked she noticed that they were heading south down Die Ellerstrasse towards the Volksgarten Park. It was getting dark when the *pfennig* dropped. Maria suddenly recalled the terrible stories about the Düsseldorf Monster, the hair went up on the back of her neck and she told the stranger that she would now find her own way to a hostel. An argument ensued. By chance, standing close by was Peter Kürten who intervened.

Even referring to Kürten's own account, piecing together what followed has not been, for me, an easy task, but it seems Maria accepted his offer of assistance when he told her that she could stay at his rooms on Mettmanner Strasse. However, when they arrived he tried his luck and propositioned her. She refused him saying that she didn't want sex and could he please find her another place to sleep. Thwarted, with his sexual urges rising with every passing minute, Kürten agreed.

Kürten later told his psychiatrist that they walked along Worringer Platz (a transit stop in Düsseldorf) and that he led the confused and very scared young woman deep into the Gräfenberg Woods where he suddenly grabbed her hand and asked, 'Can I have you?' It seems that under duress she agreed. Nevertheless, adding to his account, he went on:

> 'I thought that under the circumstances she would agree and my opinion was right. Afterwards, I took her back to the tram, but I did not accompany her right to it because I was afraid she might inform the police officer who was standing there. I had no intention of killing Budlick as she had offered no resistance.'

Be that as it may, unsurprisingly, this rape – and we should call it such – and her close call with death greatly upset Maria who returned almost immediately to Cologne where she fretted for a few days. Then, on Saturday, 17 May, she wrote a letter to her friend, a Frau Bruckner. Unbeknownst to Kürten, looming fate was intervening once again because a Frau Brugmann opened the envelope in error. She read the contents describing the rape, the man and his rooms in great detail, so the public-spirited woman contacted the police.

Ernst August Ferdinand Gennat (1880–1939) was in charge of the investigation. He was a gifted criminologist, a 'super cop' later to become *Direktor der Berliner Kriminal Polizei*, and in looking back over his career for this book, I learned something refreshingly new. I had always been led to believe that the definition of 'serial killer' was commonly attributed to former FBI Special Agent Robert Kenneth Ressler (1937–2013) who first coined the term 'serial homicide' in 1974, in a lecture at the UK's Bramshill Police College. The late author Ann Rule, however, postulated in her book *Kiss Me, Kill Me* (2004), that the credit for coining 'serial killer' goes to LAPD Detective, Pierce Brooks, who created the Violent Apprehension Programme (ViCap) system in 1985. But – oops – that's not entirely correct.

In truth it was the stolid Ernst Gennat who developed most of what we today call 'Offender Profiling'. His work is documented in articles designed for public readings, such as his 1930 paper on Peter Kürten, *Die Düsseldorfer Sexualverbrechen (The Düsseldorf Sex Crimes)*, in which Gennat becomes the very first law enforcement officer to come up with the term '*Serienmörder*' (Serial Killer), so you can take that one to the bank! However, needless to say with this Sherlock Holmes on his trail Peter Kürten's days are numbered.

When police finally tracked Maria Budlick down on Thursday, 22 May, she described a brass nameplate that read '71 Mettmanner Strasse'. Leutnant Inspektor

Ernst Gennat then persuaded her to accompany him and other officers to the address where he knocked, entered and climbed the creaking stairs to search the building for evidence. At some point Kürten spotted Maria and panicked. He tore down the stairs right past two rather lackadaisical policemen and into the street where he vanished into the night. An infuriated Gennat and his men gave chase but the nimble Kürten managed to slip away. He was on the run. Hundreds of polizei were trying to hunt him down – the hunter had become the hunted, and a determined Ernst Gennat was leading them. He was resolved to get his man.

The wily Kürten meanwhile contemplated his next move, remembering in his confession:

'Throughout the night I walked about. On Thursday 22 May, I saw my wife in the morning in the flat so I fetched my things away in a bag and rented a room in the Alderstrasse, I slept quietly until Friday morning.'

It would be fair to say that, at this stage, Kürten was confused, as might he well have been, and he made a simple but important mistake. Maria Budlick was a one-off incident as far as the police were concerned. It hadn't even crossed their minds that the man they were looking for was the man the media had dubbed 'The Düsseldorf Monster'. In fact, according to Kürten's own testimony he had convinced himself that although they most likely did not suspect him as being the serial killer it wouldn't take long before they did.

But what *if* the cops *had* suspected him? What evidence did the police have to link him to the serial killings? At first blush, it seems, not much at all. Had Kürten kept his mouth shut then there was a good probability that he would have only been charged with raping Maria Budlick and it would have been a difficult conviction to secure. Any lawyer worth his salt would have presented a defence arguing that it had been Kürten who had rescued Maria from a man making unwanted sexual advances. It had been the public-spirited Kürten who had offered to find the young woman rooms. After all was said and done, did she not agree to go with him into the woods where 'consensual sex' took place? And why did she not go straight to the police immediately afterwards? There was an officer standing next to the tram stop at Worringer Platz so why did she not report the rape there and then? Was it because she feared stigma and shame? It would all come down to her word against his. However, with the indefatigable super cop Ernst Gennat breathing down Kürten's scrawny neck and with at least half-a-dozen surviving witnesses to Kürten's rapes and attempted homicides and who had given police rough descriptions of their attacker, he was now up the River Rhine without a paddle.

'Today, 23 May, in the morning, I told my wife that I was also responsible for the Schulte affair, adding my usual remark that it would mean ten years or more separation for us, probably forever. At that, my wife was inconsolable. She spoke of unemployment, lack of means and starvation in old age. She raved that I should take my own life then she would do

the same, since her future was completely
without hope. Then, in the late afternoon,
I told my wife that I could help her.'

Peter Kürten: partial written confession

What little conscience Kürten had left now focused upon his loyal and devoted wife who had struggled through thick and thin with him for so many years. He suggested that she turn him in to collect what amounted to a very substantial reward – money enough to last her for many years. She agreed, therefore, on Saturday, 24 May, to go to the police and tell them everything. She explained that she was planning to meet Peter at 3 p.m. outside of the Rochus Kirche in Düsseldorf. When he turned up, armed officers arrested him and he went meekly into custody, saying with a wink, 'There is no need to be afraid.'

'After my head has been chopped off, will I still be able
to hear, at least for a moment, the sound of my own
blood gushing from my neck? That would be the best
pleasure to end all pleasures.'

Peter Kürten

Frau Kürten got a lengthy separation from her husband and disappeared into anonymity with the equivalent of $1,000,000, which was a very substantial sum back then (very roughly, US$15,000 or £11,500) in her handbag. For his part, Kürten got a separation too – one that separated his head from his body that is. Kürten's execution was fixed for 6 a.m., Wednesday, 2 July 1930. For his last meal he ordered Wiener schnitzel, fried potatoes and white wine. Aged just forty-eight, and accepting his fate with equanimity, he went to the guillotine with a full belly.

We will leave this chapter with the words of his psychiatrist Dr. Karl Berg:

> 'He [Kürten] was not accused of these crimes one by one, but reeled them off on his own account, beginning with number one and ending with number seventy-nine, every single case, dictating them, in fact, to the stenographer and even showing enjoyment at the horrified faces of the many police officers listening to his recital, day by day.'

['Number one' was the unknown girl left for dead by Kürten in 1899; 'Number seventy-nine' was Gertrude Bell.]

★★★

Friedrich Heinrich Karl
'Fritz' Haarmann

'Do you think I enjoy killing people? I was ill for eight days
after the first time.'

Fritz Haarmann, at his trial in December 1924

It's a strange old world is it not? We are almost
cinematically programmed to think that the most
heinous serial killers all came or come out of the USA
– but that's Hollywood, I guess. And of course we Brits
have our own history of serial murderers too. So, please
excuse me if we return again to Deutschland for the
next candidate in our top ten. For Peter Kürten was not
the only serial killer to flourish in Germany between the
wars.

As many noted writers and crime historians have
confirmed, Haarmann could easily surpass in the
number and horror of his crimes most other serial killers
past and present. Some declare that he killed at least fifty.
That is unlikely, but the twenty-eight murders to which
he confessed were accomplished in circumstances so
revolting that it would be impossible to imagine a lower
depth to which human depravity could sink. Every

homicide is a dreadful and wicked act, but there are few killers that can really hold a satanic candle to Fritz Haarmann. So, was this beast – like Peter Kürten – the Devil's spawn thus deserved of a place in Hell?

Fritz Haarmann was born in Hanover on Saturday, 25 October 1879, the sixth and youngest child to an ill-suited couple. It can be said that his parents' marriage was one of convenience for she was a wealthy woman with a substantial dowry, and her then beloved could see rich pickings for he was an unsavoury character, indeed.

The patriarch, Ollie Haarmann, a locomotive stoker, was known to everyone in the district as 'Sulky Ollie (Olle)'. He was an authoritative, morose, bullying, irritable and miserly fellow and frequently indulged in drink. He was a notorious womaniser, had several affairs throughout their marriage and later contracted syphilis. He also had little time for his children. Yet, with the patience of a saint, his wife, Johanna, would stick by him until her death in April 1901.

Johanna was seven years older than her husband, and a helpless invalid, who had taken to her bed after her youngest, Fritz, was born. Their eldest son became a respectable workman, but all the other children, including three daughters, showed unmistakable tendencies to revolt against moral law. Wilhelm, the other boy, was sent to a reformatory. We have noted already that dysfunctional childhoods, bad diet and *perhaps* bad genetic seed, can certainly turn otherwise good fruit into something rotten.

Young Fritz worshipped his mother but loathed his father. At an early age he was shy, bashful in the company of other boys, and preferred to sit by the bedside of his mother, play with his sisters' dolls and dress in their clothes. Even helping the girls with the housework delighted him. He also took an interest in needlework and cookery, and his mother doted on him. He started his schooling aged seven, where his teachers found him to be a spoiled and mollycoddled child who was prone to daydreaming. He was generally well behaved at school but did not excel academically for he was well below average and twice he had to repeat a full school year. At the age of eight, it is alleged that he was molested by one of his teachers, although he never confirmed this.

Haarmann was a physically strong teenager. With his parents' agreement, he finished his schooling in 1894 and briefly found employment as an apprentice locksmith in Neuf-Brisach – a town in the department of Haut-Rhin in the French region of Alsace – before opting in 1895, at age sixteen (some say fifteen), to enroll in a military academy for non-commissioned officers in the town of Brisach. After just five months service, he suffered an attack of sunstroke during manoeuvres. He began to suffer periodic lapses of consciousness, which although initially diagnosed as sudden signs of anxiety neurosis, would subsequently be identified as being equivalent to epilepsy, in 1895. The following year, at his own request he was released from his first stint of military service and into his father's employment.

Ollie Haarmann had a little cigar factory established in 1888. He found his son to be a lazy and inefficient worker, and the two were frequently at loggerheads. Other aspects of young Haarmann's behaviour at this time started to attract the notice of the authorities as by the age of sixteen he had started committing his first known sex offences. Haarmann had started luring young boys to secluded areas – typically cellars – where he would sexually abuse them. He was arrested in July 1896. But he didn't stop and, following further offences, the Division for Criminal Matters ordered a Dr. Gurt Schmalf (sometimes recorded as 'Schmalfuss') to examine Fritz. Schmalf came to the conclusion that the teenager was 'incurably feeble-minded' or 'incurably deranged', and therefore was unfit to stand trial. He ordered him to be confined at a mental institution indefinitely. In 1897, Haarmann was sent to Hildesheim Asylum for observation. And oh, would that he had been detained indefinitely for then German society would have been measurably safer. Several months later Haarmann escaped.

At this point in Haarmann's narrative, I begin to smell a rat and that rat is, of course, young Fritz. Here we have a juvenile, serial sex offender with a rapidly developing deviant psychopathology – an emerging psychopath – and we know that psychopaths are arch manipulators, often so-much-so that they even can fool the shrinks as history tells us. So maybe Haarmann wasn't so feeble-minded after all? Nevertheless, a fire broke out in the asylum at Christmas, 1895. It is thought that Haarmann himself, with assistance from his mother, started the blaze in order to escape. He fled to Zurich, Switzerland, where he lodged with a relative. For a while, this allegedly 'feeble-minded' young man earned a living as a handyman in a shipyard (some said he was a 'boat maker' but I think that is a little over-stating his role) and then worked for a chemist in Zurich. Nevertheless, his stay in Switzerland only lasted a mere sixteen months before he returned to Hanover in April 1899. Quite why he went back home remains unclear but, once again, life for him became a series of wrangles and fights with his father. He became engaged to a Frauline Erna Loewert, then, in October 1900, Haarmann received his call-up papers. On Friday, 12 October 1900 he was sent to the crack 10th Jäger (infantry) Battalion, in Colmar, Alsace.

In trying to dispel the notion that Haarmann was 'feeble-minded', it is worth noting that he proved to be a born soldier and an excellent marksman. He was scrupulously obedient and performed his duties with a care and thoroughness that won the praise of all his officers. He would later describe this period of service with his battalion as being the happiest of his entire life. However he fell ill with neurasthenia. Used as a psychopathological term, 'neurasthenia' denotes a condition with symptoms of: fatigue; anxiety; headaches; heart palpitations; high blood pressure; neuralgia and depressed moods. And wouldn't you have depressed moods if you had that lot fucking up your day? I know *I* would! But let's hold our horses here, because maybe that wasn't all that Fritz suffered. His discharge papers show that he suffered from 'dementia praecox' too. This is also known as 'premature dementia' or 'precocious madness' – a now disused psychiatric diagnosis that originally designated a chronic, deteriorating psychotic disorder characterised by rapid cognitive disintegration, usually beginning in the late teens or early childhood. It can cause paranoia, hallucinations and bizarre delusions. So, perhaps the last place Fritz Haarmann needed to be was behind the sights of a military rifle, or wandering around with live grenades in his pouches and high explosives close to hand. So it was a case of *Auf wiedersehen schutze (rifleman) Haarmann, verpiss dich, schnell*! He was discharged on Monday, 28 July 1902 with an excellent character reference and a monthly pension of twenty-one gold marks, which he drew until the day he was put on trial for murder in 1924.

Terrified by Fritz's violence and threats, when the youth once again returned like a bad *pfennig*, his father, now realising that the worm had turned, made a desperate and patently futile attempt to get his unruly son re-confined in a mental institution. When that didn't work, Haarmann went to live with his fiancée, Erna, in Hanover. For a short time, he worked for his father making cigars. He was sacked, but he quickly and unsuccessfully filed a maintenance lawsuit against his father, citing that he was unable to work due to the 'ailments' noted on his military discharge papers. Being a lot brighter than his son, Haarmann Sr. successfully defended the suit, which was dropped leaving the youth to pick up the bill. Out of pocket and rapidly going out of his mind, the following year, a violent fight broke out between father and son and this resulted in Haarmann Sr. himself unsuccessfully initiating legal proceedings against his son – citing verbal death threats and blackmail as justification to have his son again returned to a mental institution. The proceedings may have been unsuccessful, but Haarmann Junior was required to undergo a psychiatric evaluation.

Step forward another shrink, a Dr. Andrea, who undertook the examination of Fritz in May 1903. He sent the results to Haarmann Sr. on Thursday, 14 May confirming that his son was 'morally unstable, dull-witted, vindictive and selfish', adding 'but he is not mentally ill, so there are no grounds for sending him to a lunatic asylum'.

With the financial assistance of his father (somewhat strange considering that Haarmann Sr, had been doing all in his power to have his son thrown into a nuthouse and the key then thrown away), Fritz and his fiancée, Erna, opened a fishmonger's shop. He also briefly attempted to work as an insurance salesman before being officially classified as disabled and unable to work by the 10th Army in 1904, the result of which was that his monthly pension was slightly increased. That same year, Erna, then pregnant with Fritz's child, ended their engagement after he accused her of having an affair. The fishmonger's was owned and registered in Erna's name so she simply ordered Fritz off the premises and onto the streets. The baby was later stillborn.

There are several different accounts of what happened next in Fritz Haarmann's utterly dysfunctional narrative. What is likely the truth is that he became a wandering vagrant, con artist, hawker, burglar and petty thief during the ten years before the Great War. When he did occasionally find legitimate employment, he stole from his employers and their clients. In 1905, he served several short prison terms for larceny, embezzlement and assault. On one occasion he ingratiated himself with a female colleague whilst he was working as an invoice clerk. He would later claim that together they robbed several graves between 1905 and 1913 (he was never charged with these offences). Between the years of 1905 and 1912, Fritz Haarmann was mostly behind bars.

Haarmann's life up until this point is a mixed bag to be sure. His criminal activities meant that he was soon known in the underworld of many German cities and he was a popular figure among other petty crooks. Apparently, there was a soft side to him too for he took a genuine interest in outcasts and criminals of every kind, chatting to them for hours, lending an attentive ear to their secrets and helping them with money and advice. For their part, they regarded him as a fat, stupid but genial fellow who was ready to help them out of a hole with a few *pfennigs* whenever they needed help. Indeed, even the police began to like 'Fritzie' Haarmann. Arrested time after time, he always went quietly, laughing and joking with his captors. He seemed to actually enjoy prison where he made himself thoroughly at home and his sentences were often cut short thanks to his good conduct. A few months before the outbreak of The Great War, he was convicted of a series of thefts and frauds at a warehouse where he had been employed. The judge decided that *this* time the habitual criminal should be given a severe lesson. With a number of other offences taken into consideration, and despite his pleas of innocence, Haarmann was sentenced to a custodial term of five years.

War began in July the following year and compulsory conscription began to literally drain fit and able-bodied German men from society to fight for the country to leave a great shortage of available domestic manpower at home. So, it may come as no surprise to learn that during his final years of penal servitude Haarmann was given day release to work in the grounds of several manor houses near the town of Rendsburg while under strict orders to return to prison each evening.

Emerging from confinement in April 1918, Fritz Haarmann, now aged thirty-nine, first moved to Berlin, before deciding to return to his roots in Hanover. There, he briefly lived with one of his sisters before renting a single room apartment in the August of the same year.

To put Haarmann's crimes into context, we have to acknowledge that the interwar years were ones of tremendous upheaval in Germany. The country was now at peace, but plunged into a moral anarchy that was, in many ways, more soul-destroying than war. Germany had suffered huge territorial losses and had to give away swathes of land and population to Poland, Russia, France and Denmark. Ultimately, the country had to sign the Treaty of Versailles – the whole country was effectively on the bones of its ass. With the exile of the Kaiser after Germany's defeat in the First World War, a Republican constitution was drawn up at Weimar in 1919. The new government was liberal in tone, but always struggled with the burden of huge war debts, a resentful, demoralised populace and an industrial base that was in the hands of just a few individuals. There were attempted coups by both the right and the left. Added to this, rampant inflation was destroying the economy. In January 1922, the exchange rate was 162 marks to the dollar: two years later one dollar bought 4,200 billion marks. There were food riots and the government was forced to take austerity measures. These worked for a time, but when the Great Depression of 1929–31 hit, Germany was affected particularly badly. When the ill-fated Weimar Republic crumbled, Hitler eventually took power in 1933.

In post-war Germany, the profiteer, the swindler and the crook were reigning in open triumph over the ruins of law, order and honesty. It was a world that Haarmann fitted right into, saying later at this trial:

> 'I went to Berlin. Then I came back to Hanover, and so to my sister Emma's. Bertchen, her youngest, says to me, "Don't eat too much bread, uncle. We have to snake (queue) up for it. We're all ill." Says I, "I'll go and have a look, kid, what's to be done." So then I went to the Hof railway station. Emma gave me some cash. Talking about profiteers and hagglers! That's where they were indeed. We had a good talk. I got everything there. We all got fat again with what I got.'

Haarmann was in his element amongst this den of thieves, establishing several criminal contacts with whom he could trade in contraband and stolen property. Out of the misery of the war, Hanover had grown a great sprawling market near the railway station. Here, at myriad ramshackle stalls, even the very poorest could buy a host of half-hitched or otherwise doubtful wares: sawdust bread; coffee; second-hand clothes; trinkets; margarine; furniture and meat – sometimes of cats and dogs – and so on. And, inside the great station lived an army of the unemployed, the homeless, labourers, tramps, fugitives, refugees, and, of course, crooks and thieves. Most of this population consisted of young boys who had run away from homes; rebelled against their fathers who had returned from the front; or come in search of work or adventure in the chaos of the new Germany. So, there they all were, crouching around the stoves by day, and huddling together on the platform benches at night. In the midst of this once fairy-tale town with its gabled roofs and winding alleys had arisen a jungle through which prowled the scum of the earth and it was here that Fritz Haarmann got fat again, because now, it was Fritzie's killing time!

> 'Oh, what a tangled web we weave,
> when first we practise to deceive.'
> *Sir Walter Scott (1771–1832).*

When Haarmann first entered the Hof station of Hanover that night in 1918, he knew instinctively that here was the world in which he could earn a comfortable livelihood. For the time being he didn't worry about *how* he was going to do that. Instead he chatted – in the genial way that seemed to make strangers take to him instantly – with the outcasts he saw everywhere around him. The vulnerable, pale, blue-lipped youngsters that huddled around the stoves interested him most of all and soon he found himself questioning them closely. It struck him as most remarkable that there, for the first time in a country where everyone had been so carefully documented, were groups of human beings passing through the station in a never-ending flow – humans whom no one would be able to trace if they happened to disappear.

Can you see Haarmann now, because there he is, standing over a bunch of the wide-eyed and hungry? For him, they are simply money in his grubby pocket. Many had run away from their homes, usually in distant towns and washed up here. Neither parents nor the police had the slightest inkling of the whereabouts of these disenfranchised youngsters.

In the days that followed, Haarmann took a lodging at 27 Cellarstrasse – the street still exists today. Here he set up in business as a meat hawker and seller of old clothes. This shrewd villain had a keen eye for a bargain and he could beat the market hagglers at their own game, so he soon began to prosper. All of which may give further doubt to the idea that he was 'feeble-minded'. Now established amongst some of the canniest crooks in Hanover, Haarmann was brighter than a policeman's whistle.

A police official approached Haarmann one night. He knew that Fritz was a jailbird, and the officer had noted with a canny eye how easily this bluff, garrulous peddler gained the confidence of the shiftiest in the station. Taking Haarmann into a quiet corner, the officer whispered in Fritz's ear: 'Why don't you work for us?' Streetwise Haarmann cottoned on instantly. Crime was so rife in Hanover during those years of unrest that the police – poorly paid and overstretched – were unable to make any headway against it without the aid of an army of 'narks' or police spies. There wasn't any money in the coffers to pay these informers. In return for their 'services' they were granted a certain measure of immunity for their own offences against the law. The police turned the blind eye – or perhaps they closed their eyes – when a 'nark' was robbing or swindling. Of course, the police had not a clue that they were effectively giving Haarmann a licence to kill. They could have no idea of the nature of the crimes he would now go on to commit.

Fritz avidly seized the chance offered to him. Within a few weeks he was a familiar figure in every police station with his tales of criminal plots – some real, some bogus – being hatched. He had acquired a vast and intimate knowledge of Hanover's underworld, which he never hesitated to use against his friends, confidants and competitors in his attempts to curry more favour with the police. They say that there is no honour amongst thieves and Haarmann certainly fitted the bill, again suggesting that he wasn't as dimwitted as previously believed. Oh, what a tangled web we weave, when we first practise to deceive, for soon he was known everywhere as 'Detective Haarmann'.

His business as a 'meat vendor' was also flourishing. The *hausfrauen* liked to buy from him because he was 'in with the police'. Also, not only was his meat much cheaper (which could be because he was closing down his competitors) he could be relied upon and considered a genial, trustworthy hail-fellow-well-met.

Welfare workers came to know Fritz. It warmed their hearts when they saw him approach a group of homeless boys at the station, laughing and joking with them, distributing bars of chocolate and packs of cigarettes. These kids came to the station in droves; train-jumpers from towns hundreds of miles away, hungry, grimy and forlorn. He would shake an exhausted youngster by the shoulders, gruffly demand his papers, listen to the lad's tearful explanations with an air of frowning disbelief, then his round, shiny face would break into a friendly grin and he would cackle: '*Komm mit mir Junge und ich werde dir eine mahlzeit und eine matratze besorgen.*' ('Come with me boy and I'll find you a meal and a mattress.') Thereafter, the young boy would simply disappear and some of him would end up in someone's stew.

During the six years between 1918 and 1924, rumours grew throughout Northern Germany that Hanover was becoming a town with a sinister reputation. The narrow streets and fetid houses of the old quarter had long been notorious as warrens where ne'er-do-wells thrived, but now one newspaper after another began to notice that Hanover was a modern Labyrinth of Crete, into which youths entered never to be seen again. In fact, it was estimated by one paper that during a twelve-month period more than six hundred youngsters who had left their homes in northern towns had been traced to Hanover – but no further. Public disquiet began to spread. There were queer goings-on in this Dickensian type of old town. A wild terror, which the authorities were unable to stifle, began to spread among the inhabitants, compounded when a newspaper report concluded that a werewolf was roaming the town by night, rending and devouring anyone in its path. 'Der Werwolf von Hannover' became legend whispered by locals who spoke of children being butchered in cellars, their bones thrown into the River Leine. Every now and then there was an outbreak of hysteria among people who had bought suspicious-tasting meat, and the police were kept very busy examining portions brought to them by white-faced *fraus*. Goodness gracious me. We might think that our Victorian 'Jack the Ripper' was a bad egg, but he doesn't hold a candle to Fritzie does he? The authorities did all they could to reassure the distracted populace, and reams of letters from crime and medical experts were published in the newspapers scoffing at this mass neurosis. It was a conspiracy, fake news they argued. One can imagine if this happened in today's world with the internet. Oh, dear me, the shit would truly hit the proverbial fan!

The rumours refused to be quelled and they rose ominously on Saturday, 17 May 1924, when kiddies playing on the banks of the slow-moving River Leine found a human skull. Twelve days later another small skull, apparently of a young boy, was found, and on Friday, 13 June (grim date indeed) two more skulls started staring at passersby.

In a pathetic effort to mitigate the fear caused by discoveries of these human artifacts, one doctor said he thought that medical students had been playing jokes. Another doctor declared that the skulls had probably floated down the river some fifty kilometres from Alfeld, where a plague of typhus was causing hurried and perhaps inadequate burials. But now the slight wind of panic had risen to one of gale-force proportions and it swept before it any such considerations. *Mein Gott*! On Thursday, 24 July, boys playing in a meadow near the River Leine found a sack of human bones and the *menschen*, now frantic with fear, clamoured for action. Watched by a crowd of thousands from the banks, dredgers set to work in the sombre river, reaching down into its murky depths and black ooze. Night fell. Huge searchlights were erected pointing shafts of intense light into the secret depths. At this point I would like to be able to say that they found *nicht*, but I can't. Within twenty-four hours some five hundred human bones were brought to the surface. There are only just over two hundred bones in one human body. Of course, we don't know what size of bones they actually were, but

I suspect they must have been quite substantial ones and would have discounted the three smallest bones – the malleus, incus and stapes, which are just three to five millimetres in size. But five hundred human bones *were* counted – *not* nice work if you can get it.

Friday, 27 September 1918 was the day that seventeen-year-old Friedel Rothe disappeared. The lad was in big trouble. He had sold the civilian clothes belonging to his father, a soldier, who was now on his way home from the front. Fearing his anger, Friedel was too scared to return home. And you can understand how wild his father had cause to be considering the circumstances. Probably missing a limb or two, the bedraggled Unteroffizier Rothe was praying that somehow he would manage to get himself home after a few years wading around in waterlogged trenches being shot at and he would have been hoping to take a bath, put on a clean shirt and Y-fronts... then a letter came from Frau Rothe informing him that his son had nicked everything, socks, shoes and his Y-fronts too. Wouldn't you be furious if that had happened to you...? I know I would be. I mean if my lad misappropriated my lederhosen I would go ape!

Nonetheless, Friedel was spotted near the station market in Hanover by a family friend, one Paul Montag. Two days later his mother received a postcard from her boy: 'Dear Mother. It is more than two days since I ran away. But I will only come home if you promise to be kind to me. Affectionate greetings, your son, Fritz.' That very day Herr Rothe returned home from the war and both parents immediately began to look for their son. It was a search that would prove to become Haarmann's undoing.

Paul Montag explained that he had seen Friedel going about with a 'fine gentleman' who had given him presents and taken him for a ride in the park. Friedel had boasted to Paul, 'I have been to his room. There we smoke and amuse ourselves.' The parents made further enquiries and discovered that Friedel had been seen in a billiards room with 'Detective Haarmann'. They went to the police and demanded an immediate search of Haarmann's lodgings – 27 Cellarstrasse.

At first the police would not listen to the Rothes' pleadings. Haarmann was one of their 'star' men, currently unearthing a new communist conspiracy or gang of thieves almost every day. It was ridiculous that a man so valuable and highly trusted should be subjected to such an indignity merely because of a foolish and unfounded suspicion. For his part, decorated soldier, Unteroffizier Rothe, had been subjected to the horrors of war, certainly not a man to be trifled with, nor one to be fobbed off by a few petty officials or police officers. He put his foot down, resorted to threats and almost to force before he persuaded police to go with him and search Haarmann's premises. Upon their arrival they caught 'Detective Haarmann' with his trousers down and in the company of a semi-naked thirteen-year-old boy. He was charged with both sexual assault and battery of a minor, and sentenced to nine months imprisonment. Alas, the police didn't look through his rooms very thoroughly for, at his trial six years later, Haarmann chuckled: 'When the police examined my room, the head of the boy, Friedel, was lying wrapped in newspaper behind the oven.' Haarmann had escaped a murder charge by the skin of his teeth.

Upon his release, Haarmann moved into Nikolaistrasse and met Hans Grans, then just twenty years old. Grans was to play an eerie role in the career of this serial killer. He was a slim and graceful youth, cynical, indolent, and self-possessed, with a good brain and a heart of ice. He belonged to a higher level of society than Haarmann and had attended a secondary school and came from a good home where his parents, who kept a lending library in Hanover, tried to instill into him some principles of culture and morality. Despite all of this, Hans had run away from home and was just the sort of young outcast whom Haarmann had marked out as his especial prey – a better quality of well-reared German meat, if we can put it this way. He was soon to become Haarmann's lover and an accomplice in murder most foul. Haarmann had now met his match. From the very beginning of their acquaintance the younger, classier Hans had the ascendancy over the ill-bred Haarmann, lashing him into a frenzy with his sarcasm, taunting him until he brought the killer weeping to his knees. In fact, upon reflection, Hans would have made good SS officer material in World War II, such an arrogant chap he was. He was the very sort one would have enjoyed watching being hung after the Nuremberg Trials. 'You lump!' he would sneer into the abject, slobbering face of Haarmann. 'You slaughterer!'

The gossip that would come to envelop Hanover began. Just whispers and curtain-twitching at first, you must understand. Strange tales started to circulate about Fritz and Hans, so they upped sticks and moved into the Neuestrasse, then into the Rothe Reihe (Red Row), an alley that ran through the ghetto of the old town on the bank of the dark River Leine, yet still they could not shake off the whispering that followed them. There seemed to be a constant procession of young lads going into the rooms of the Rothe Reihe apartment – but never coming out again – and noises of chopping and splashing and occasional muffled screams. Now and again grief-stricken parents came searching for their missing sons, whom they heard had last been seen with 'Detective Haarmann'. Sometimes the police accompanied them, but always they departed no wiser than when they arrived.

Notwithstanding, neighbours had now begun to grow even more suspicious and alarmed. For instance, one Frau Engel met Haarmann on their shared staircase carrying a bucket over which was spread a newspaper. Invariably the meat hawker stopped to gossip and joke with her and when the paper moved aside she saw the bucket was full of blood. She was horrified for a moment, but later thought no more of it. After all, it was part of Haarmann's trade to hack up carcasses of smuggled meat, and he always ensured Frau Engel had the best cuts at the lowest prices anyway. And when police called upon him with anxious parents in tow? Well, that was because the police often came to him for assistance when they were looking for a missing lad. Nothing suspicious about that at all! And, hey, the cops were always given a very special cut of free meat after all was said and done.

Then there was Frau Seeman; a dim-witted person who lived in the room below Haarmann. She called out to him one day when she heard him chopping and shouted, 'Am I going to get a bit?' Instantly, Haarmann replied, 'No, next time'. If anything, Fritz was a cunning man for the next day he brought her a parcel of bones. She considered making soup out of them, but thought that the bones looked too white so she threw them away. Making no bones about it, time was running out for Fritz Haarmann, as more suspicions began to arise. A piece of flesh he sold to a Frau Brotschecken appeared so strange to her that she took it to the police doctor for analysis. He told her that it was 'pork'.

A Frau Becke bought stockings for her son from Haarmann, whose stock of second-hand clothes seemed suddenly to have increased tenfold. She found two spots of blood on them and threw them away – the need to request a refund not crossing her mind.

A worker named Busch noticed that a boy who was always in the Hof railway station, and who wore a suit of peculiar texture, had suddenly disappeared. A few days later he saw Hans wearing the same suit!

A Franz Mrotzeck passed Haarmann's room one afternoon. The door was open and he spied a young boy lying very still on the bed, with his face turned to the wall. 'Ah, yes... hush, don't disturb him,' whispered Haarmann. 'He is asleep, the poor lad. He needs sleep you understand.' The door was then closed. Later the sound of chopping started all over again.

To all intents and purposes, Fritz Haarmann seemed to be living a charmed life, and, if he had had the wits to stop his killing spree at this point, in all likelihood he would never have been caught. Indeed, he seemed so sure of his protection by the police as a leading snitch that he took incredible risks. He openly hawked the clothes and small articles owned by his victims a day or two after murdering them – that is to say when these possessions were not claimed by Hans Grans, who had first pick as his part of the proceeds of Haarmann's evil doings. Perks of the job, if you will? But after the aforementioned sack of bones had been found in the meadow near the Leine, the reports, that were now widespread about the monster of Rothe Reihe, forced the authorities to take action. Hitherto, they had kept their suspicions to themselves. Now, however, they had to reckon, not with an occasional distracted parent, but with a furious general public and a press greedy for headlines. They needed to take instant and drastic action.

The Chief of the Hanover Police was caught between a rock and a hard place. Haarmann was now something like bent nobility for by now he was a prominent recruiter for the 'Black Reichswehr': the organisation, which, with the secret approval of the authorities, was working against the French occupation of the Ruhr. Hanover's Polizeichef knew that scores of his officers were turning a blind eye to Haarmann's black market activities while other police officers were complicit and actively benefitting from it. Moreover, in partnership with a highly placed police official, Haarmann had established a private detective bureau called the 'Lasso Agency'. An accusation against someone who had made himself so useful to the authorities as Fritz Haarmann might – if it proved false – have very serious implications, and *die scheisse wurde den fan treffen* (the shit would hit the fan).

Faced with this distasteful dilemma, and after much considerable hesitation, the chief of police decided to pass the buck and sent to Berlin for two detectives with whom Haarmann was *not* personally acquainted. They were instructed to shadow the movements of Haarmann at the Hof railway station. On the evening of Sunday, 22 June 1924 the old lag accosted an ungainly, quarrelsome fifteen-year-old named Karl Fromm. The Berlin detectives seized the opportunity of the ensuing argument to arrest both of them.

Back at the police station, while Fromm was making voluble accusations against Haarmann, claiming that he'd been raped and assaulted for some days by the man at his flat. The police hurried to Haarmann's rooms in the Rothe Reihe. Here they found the walls splashed and splattered with blood, all indicating that some animal – or *someone* – had been butchered. They discovered a heap of clothing and other articles that later proved to be damning evidence against this serial killer. When the investigators returned to the police station and confronted Haarmann, he protested his innocence – '*Nein, nein, ich bin unschuldig,*' – claiming that the bloodstains were present due to his trade as a butcher and seller of meat. The clothes, trinkets and so on were his stock as a secondhand dealer, he explained. But when the mother of one of the missing boys identified the coat worn by her son, the cops began to put Haarmann through the third degree. Eventually he broke down and confessed to some twenty-four homicides although the true number could exceed that greatly. Then, to prove that there is absolutely no honour amongst thieves, he accused Hans Grans as instigator and accomplice. Grans was instantly arrested.

Their MO proves for disturbing reading so let us not allow the passage of time to dilute the horror of it all. Exhibiting very loose parallels with the MOs of the now executed, American serial killer John Wayne Gacy (1942–1994) and the UK's deceased, necrophile, serial murderer Dennis Nilsen (1945–2018), Haarmann and Grans would visit the Hof railway station at night to select a suitable victim from the hordes of young, disenfranchised young men and boys who sat shivering and bewildered in the waiting rooms and on the platform benches. Haarmann would play the friendly missioner, anxious to give the lad a hot meal and a comfortable bed. If this bluff did not work, the educated Grans, who could be very charming and persuasive, usually succeeded in winning the boy's confidence. The two were acting as a tag team – a killing tag team – much in the same way as the partnership between Fred and Rosemary West or Ian Brady and Myra Hindley. Sometimes, however, Haarmann had to resort to bullying, pretending to be dissatisfied with the lad's identity papers; flashing the stamped pass he carried as a member of the 'Lasso Detective Service' and, finally, using his authority as an unofficial police agent to summon the railway police to his aid if the boy still remained suspicious and disobedient. This despicable German couple merely saw the lads as commodities, nothing more, nothing less, and the more time they wasted picking one up the more risk they placed themselves in. Once they had successfully ensnared their prey, Haarmann would take the lad back to his rooms, rape, kill him and hack up the body. The next day he hawked the victim's clothing and other small possessions in the market outside the station.

The trial of Haarmann and Grans began at Hanover Assizes on Thursday, 4 December 1924. It lasted fourteen days, and 130 witnesses were called. Haarmann's guilt was already established. There were three main questions before the court. How many murders had Haarmann committed? Did he sell the flesh of his victims as meat? What part did Grans play in the murders?

To anyone conversant with the atmosphere of a British murder trial the scenes in that Hanover court must have appeared almost incredible. From the outset Haarmann was allowed to behave with astounding freedom, interrupting the proceedings whenever he thought fit. Indeed, when the prosecutor finished his opening speech, Haarmann called; '*Das geht doch ganz gut, nicht*!' ('You're doing fine!').

When the prosecutor questioned him about a party he had given to some friends, he asked, 'Where did you get the meat to entertain your guests?' Haarmann turned to the press box. 'Now he's really getting down to it,' he chuckled, producing a few sniggers coming from the public gallery.

'Are you a political spy?' he was quickly asked in an effort to regain control. Haarmann, grinning from ear-to-ear, replied, '*Nicht*! I have never bothered my head about politics. In fact I don't know what politics is.' The prosecutor adjusted his pince-nez, took out a spotless white handkerchief and theatrically blew his nose. He asked the clerk for several exhibits which were handed to him. He then held aloft a green school cap and a pair of braces that had belonged to Ernest Ehrenberg, a thirteen-year-old lad.

'Did you kill Ernest?' he demanded.

'Yes, that might well be,' answered Haarmann, carelessly.

'Paul Bronischewski, too, was one of your victims?'

Haarmann knitted his brows. 'I'm not sure about that one,' he replied sheepishly.

'How did you kill your victims?'

A shudder ran through the packed court as Haarmann said coolly: 'I bit them through their throats.'

The prosecutor showed him a photograph of fifteen-year-old Herman Wolf, who had vanished soon after he had boasted to friends that he knew a detective at the Hof station. Haarmann not only denied responsibility but turned towards the anguished father, sneered and said:

'I have my tastes after all. I should never have looked twice at such an ugly monster, as, according to his photographs, your son must have been. You say your boy had not even a shirt to his name, and that his socks were tied onto his feet with string. Deuce take it, you should have been ashamed to let him go out like that. There's plenty of rubbish like him around. Think what you're saying, man. Such a fellow would have been far beneath my notice.'

'How many victims did you kill altogether?' pressed the prosecutor. Haarmann pondered as if trying to do the calculations in his head. 'It might have been thirty, it might be forty... I can't really remember the exact number.' However, he again protested hotly when he was accused of the murder of schoolboy, Franz Brinkman. 'I never knew him,' he cried out. 'I won't lie. But what I haven't done, I won't admit.'

When a testifying witness hesitated, he shouted, 'Come on, old chap, you must tell us all you know. We are here to get the truth!' One morning he flew into a rage because there were so many women in the court. 'Why are all these women here?' he snapped at the judges. 'This is a case for men to discuss.' One of the judges answered apologetically, 'The law permits women to attend the court, and I have no power to alter it.' When the mother of one lad could hardly speak for grief and was a long time giving her evidence, Haarmann grew so bored that he asked the judges to let him smoke a cigar. Permission was granted immediately.

Not until the question of Grans' complicity was discussed did Haarmann lose his composure. His high-pitched voice quavered with chagrin as he cried in court: 'Grans should tell you how shabbily he has treated me. I did the murders. For that work he is too young. But he knows more than I do. I have always been his tool.' Who knows what prompted this but Haarmann exculpated his accomplice by explaining that Grans left him alone to do the murders during the night and returned the next morning to take some garment or two that he coveted. This happened in the case of Fritz Wittig, a young travelling salesman whom Grans had persuaded Haarmann to approach because he wanted the suit he was wearing.

'I just cut the body up when there was a knock at the door,' Haarmann recalled. 'I shoved the body under the bed and opened the door. It was Grans. His first question was, "Where is the suit?" I sat on the bed and buried my face in my hands. "What is the matter with me?" I moaned. "Why am I so pale, and yet a man?

Have I two souls?"... Grans tried to console me, and said: *"Man muss auch uber Leichen gehen*! (Don't let a little thing like a corpse upset you)".'

But then, in a complete volte-face, Haarmann suddenly accused Grans and a friend of his called Hugo Wittowski of the murder of young Adolf Henjes, whose overcoat was found in the rooms in the Rothe Reihe. Grans, he added, incited him to commit a number of the murders such as Wittig and also of Adolf Hannapel, aged seventeen, whose new trousers took Grans' fancy.

The trial lasted two weeks and featured a seemingly never-ending procession of parents entering the witness box to identify possessions belonging to their sons that had mysteriously found their way into Haarmann's lodgings. Dr. Brandt, who had examined Haarmann in 1911, appeared in the witness box to say that Haarmann was mentally sound and not as 'feeble-minded' as he'd previously thought. Dr. Schultz of Gottingen University declared the serial killer was 'fully responsible'. Their testimony delighted Haarmann, who all his life feared being confined in a madhouse. 'Behead me!' he had shouted during the early days of the trial. 'But don't send me to the asylum.'

Haarmann's day of judgement came on Friday, 19 December 1924. That day everyone who entered the court was searched for weapons. Haarmann glanced wildly around a court packed to suffocation, but so tensely silent at that moment that one could have heard a pin drop. Between him and the aghast spectators were twelve police officers carrying loaded revolvers. They never took their eyes off the curious throng, for an anonymous letter had arrived threatening to shoot this monster standing in the dock. Haarmann shouted:

'Condemn me to death. I only ask for justice. I am not mad. It is true I often get into a state when I do not know what I am doing. But that is not madness. Make it short. Make it soon. Deliver me from this life, which is a torment. I will not petition for mercy, nor will I appeal. I want to pass just one more merry evening in my cell with coffee, cheese and cigars, after which I will curse my father, and go to my execution as if it were a wedding!'

Although a charge of cannibalism was never proved, Haarmann was found guilty of twenty-four murders and condemned to death. His accomplice, Grans, drew a death sentence too, but Haarmann's subsequent changing testimony gave Grans the chance of an appeal. His sentence was reduced to penal servitude for life, and then later reduced to twelve years. Upon his release from prison, the once notorious killer's accomplice lived out the Nazi regime in Hanover – maybe he eventually did join Hitler's SS, but we will never know for he disappeared into obscurity. Haarmann was beheaded by guillotine in the grounds of Hanover Prison on the morning of 15 April 1925.

Thus ended a reign of terror that seemed to belong to the 'Middle Ages', but happened only a few short years ago in a civilisation undermined by the ravages of war. So what are we to make of Fritz Haarmann? Was he more evil than Peter Kürten or of lesser foulness? I think that we must agree that he earns a special place in this book – and in Hell, too. And, what of his psychopathology? A sexually depraved monster of the highest degree – of course he was. Was he as simple-minded as suggested by the earlier psychiatric diagnosis that the doctors initially agreed upon? I think not. I say this because once a person becomes, or *is* 'simple-minded' (because they are mentally wired up to be this way) he or she is that way for life. It's a shocking thing to say, but you cannot teach a person of limited intelligence to become an astronaut, a brain surgeon, a rocket scientist or even a politician. Oops, strike the latter because there are, of course, so many politicians who do live in a world where lead balls bounce, pink elephants fly and fairies reign supreme – take Donald Trump as a glittering example.

I reinforce this by stating that Fritzie was, without *any* doubt, a criminal psychopath, and these types can *never* be cured of their psychopathy – unless one executes them that is! Furthermore, as all of us with a deep interest in serial killers know all too well, these people have no feelings toward their fellow man. They are extreme narcissists, born liars, arch manipulators, control freaks and, more often than not, more cunning than any town fox.

When we study the likes of Haarmann, we should do so as dispassionately as we can – as if we are studying a blowfly preserved in amber under a microscope. It is the way I approach each and every killer I have interviewed and corresponded with over the decades. It may seem a galling thing to say, but these morally upended humans – if we can presume to call them human beings – are the scum of the earth but also morbidly fascinating. They are not social animals as we see our fellow humans. They are society's bottom-feeders, disgusting in every sense. Yet they provide us with fodder for debate, arguments and scenarios about the nature of humanity and morality. Men like Fritz Haarmann force us to bend our minds to comprehend them – 'How the holy fuck did this beast metamorphose from an innocent, newborn baby, into something so sick and morally twisted?' Was it nature or nurture? Was it nature *and* nurture? Or was he the Devil's seed? I will let my readers be the judge of that!

I'd like to finish by making some comments on Haarmann's capacity for deception. He was able to fool pretty much everyone he came across. How *can* a so-called simple-minded individual become so devious, so beguiling, so plausible, so controlling that no one really suspected he was capable of killing at all? I think that in our more enlightened times – and given the pervading lawless climate of Germany after the Great War – these days we would spot such a beast prowling amongst us much quicker and have him apprehended. In the UK we are now able to do this quite effectively. Our small geographical boundaries are of assistance to us here. In the US serial killers can often roam free, travelling through state after state and it often takes decades to catch them and bring to them their just desserts. I have written extensively about the 'masks of normality' these killers wear. These murderous Dr. Jekyll and Mr Hyde types, and my two bestsellers *Talking with Psychopaths and Savages: A Journey into the Evil Mind*, and *Talking with Psychopaths and Savages: Beyond Evil*, will take you even deeper into the dark abyss where nightmares tragically *do* come true.

So, now we move back to the Gates of Hell to find another candidate worthy of recognition amongst the Legion of the Damned.

Have you enjoyed the trip thus far because things do get worse, says I.

★★★

Theodore Robert 'Ted' Bundy

'I don't feel guilty for anything… I feel sorry for people
who feel guilt… I'm a cold-hearted sonofabitch.'

Ted Bundy

Dr. David Holmes is a renowned criminologist and
forensic psychologist – and he really *does* know his stuff.
Although David and I have never met, we both consulted
and appeared on the *Born to Kill* television series, he being
what our American cousins call the 'anchor'. Amongst the
serial killers explored in the series we had the arrogant,
egoistical, narcissist, Dr. Harold Shipman, the killing tag
teams of Myra Hindley and Ian Brady, and Fred and Rose
West. It was Dr. Holmes who coined the phrase, 'Less
than dead', when referring to these serial murderers – or
any serial killer for that matter. He explained that these
killers treat their victims as utterly disposable by-products
of their sado-sexual homicidal perversions. They were
people who would hardly be missed, and even if they were
slightly missed it wouldn't really matter.

I have interviewed face-to-face and or corresponded
with some thirty of these types of killers in my time and

they are fascinating to observe up close and personal. Sometimes they are meek, pathetic whining low lifes. Other times they are cocky, self-assured braggarts who revel in discussing their crimes. And sometimes they become so angry that their hatred radiates towards you like heat from a hot kitchen stove. Never once did any of these beasts show any genuine remorse for their victims or the devastation they caused to the next-of-kin. If one of them did shed a tear they were clearly those of a crocodile. If you were to study their body language and their facial expressions, one can readily see that they are pretending.

Several times I interviewed on camera and audio the now executed Connecticut serial killer, Michael Bruce Ross (1959–2005). In fact Michael was the first serial killer I ever met in the flesh. He was quite a likeable, bookish fellow to chat to at first. But when I asked about one of his victims he replied, 'I took her. I raped her. I killed her and I dumped the body like so much trash,' adding, 'so what else do ya'll want to fuckin' know?'

For my part, I believe that the phrase 'Less than dead' has two intertwined meanings when it comes to Michael Ross. The first is the way Ross treated his victims. The second being specifically the way he viewed his choice of victim. To Ross the young thoroughly decent girls were there to be used, abused and destroyed. There are parallels in other serial murders there. 'Carers' Cathy May Wood and Gwendoline Graham suffocated five elderly residents of their Michigan care home. I have interviewed both women on camera for the TV series *The Serial Killers*. To this killing couple, their victims were on their last legs anyway so why not simply help them on their way and have some perverted fun while we are about it. To them they were 'Less than dead' you see!

Do we not see this murderous psychopathology running like thin, steel wire through the crimes committed by Peter Kürten and Fritz Haarmann? Yes, of course we do, and this is precisely why I have started this book with chapters on these two monsters. They provide us with a psychopathological road map by which to judge the others who will make our list. All serial killers treat their victims as less than dead for they use them, abuse them, kill them and dump their bodies like so much trash! So how do we judge Theodore Robert Bundy (1946–1989) against Peter Kürten and Fritz Haarmann, for surely Ted *does* deserve a place in Hell, too?

As I said, there is no honour amongst thieves but there is some kind of honour between the 'Dead Men Walking' on the so-called 'Green Mile'. There is an inmate hierarchy in every custodial level of any so-called 'correctional facility', and the rapists and killers of innocent young kiddies are the pits – the scum. This is more-or-less why – *and* while this is an awful thing to suggest – many of us regard the likes of Dr. Shipman as being of a lesser evil than Ian Brady and Myra Hindley. So please think about that for a few moments. Putting some dear old lady to a peaceful death using lethal doses of diamorphine 'seems' a 'lesser' way to kill than the way Brady and Hindley enticed impressionable youngsters into their inescapable web, tortured then killed them to dump their pathetic bodies out there on the bleak Saddleworth Moor where they hoped that no one would find them. Okay, throw me into the stocks and pelt me with past-their-sell-by-date tomatoes and rotten eggs, but *if* we are to examine the minds of these serial killers, one has to be as dispassionate as one can be... maybe? Therefore, from the outset I was somewhat reluctant to even include Ted Bundy in this book. Therefore, I have no wish to insult the seasoned True Crime reader by reminding you who and what Bundy was. Without any doubt, he was – still is – the most talked about, written about, gossiped about, motion-pictured-about, and documented homicidal sexual predator in world history. Indeed, there is hardly ever a movie produced about serial killers these days without something of Ted's MO in it someplace. When I give my lectures and talks on serial killers and ask the audience who Ted Bundy was, all hands reach for the sky, all of which makes me feel a bit of a prat as I wonder why I ask such a dumb question in the first place. However, when my audience is heavily dotted with grey rinses from some church's knit-one-purl-one circle – average age eighty plus – and they know who 'Ted' was, something very interesting happens because stoutly comes back this sort of stuff. 'He was such a nice looking, clever young man. He drove a Volkswagen like my grandson Malcolm's got. I wrote to Ted a few times. I knitted him a sweater for his last Christmas... but he never replied.' Bundy didn't *look* like a monster. And this fact has meant that he holds a grim fascination in the minds of society.

Bundy kidnapped, raped and murdered – mostly by bludgeoning – at least thirty young girls and women during the seventies. His list of victims is thought to be much higher and his crimes are thought to have started much earlier. Before his execution at Starke Prison, Florida, on Tuesday, 24 January 1989, he confessed to thirty kills committed in seven states but the total will never be known. Bundy was highly intelligent and handsome – although whether you agree with that opinion is your call. Yes, he was well groomed, lean and attractive in a slick, oily American-car-salesman sort of way, but there is a black and white photograph of him with a Miss Carol Bartholomew at a 1975 party where he has the face of a smug rubber duck. Perhaps the best picture, the one that shows the real nature of the beast, was taken at trial and portrays a crazed howling ape, mouth agape, teeth bared with a hand poised ready to strike. Quite a terrifying sight altogether. And yet, even as he was on trial for these horrific murders of young women, hundreds upon hundreds of grossly stupid women – murder groupies – desperately tried to win his affections, offered him their hands in marriage and wanted to bear his child. Yes, superficially Bundy appeared to be a charming man, but under the surface lay an overpowering sexual urge and a pathological rage against women.

I like the adverb 'superficially' very much. It pertains to the outward appearance hiding what is beneath. Most, if not *all*, serial killers appear on the surface to be as normal as anyone else. As my loyal readers will know, I am fond of making simple analogies and here I ask you to compare him with the iceberg that sank the RMS *Titanic*. There it was floating around quite happily and minding its own business with just its icy head above water when out of the mist loomed this great ship. At first blush, to the ship's crew, the berg looked a trifling thing and a quick change of the ship's course seemed appropriate… then WALLOP! A ship-destroying monster lurked beneath the waves. Compare this to Ted Bundy, the archetypal serial killer freely moving around society seeming as innocuous as pretty much anyone else… then into his sights came prey. He lures with a fast line of chat and then the trap snaps shut on his victim and her last look is into the eyes of the crazed Bundy. The iceberg, as the *Titanic* plunged to its watery mass grave, moved calmly on its way. And so did Bundy – his heart as cold as ice and without a care in the world. When we study serial killers, we must always remember the superficiality of the surface because what hides behind this mask of normality is something we should all dread.

There are, undoubtedly, other reasons that Ted Bundy has become the most talked about serial killer in the west. He escaped from custody twice in daredevil fashion. He also represented himself during trial. Here we find a man whose other basic drive was a craving to be famous. He was the stereotype extreme narcissist and sociopath and yet, embedded in his psychopathology, he harboured a low self-esteem. Subconsciously, or perhaps even consciously, he loathed himself for what he was and all that he would ever be. There was a streak of self-pity in him, a feeling that the world was against him, preventing him from making the kind of effort that might have brought him success. I've written extensively about this in other books. It is a way of transferring blame for one's own shortcomings onto something or someone else – a form of self-mitigation, if you prefer? To use a simple analogy: a man is hammering a nail into a wall and his missus calls out 'Hey, I have told you twice, your dinner is getting cold!' The guy misses the nail and flattens his thumb, before shouting, 'Shut the fuck up, now look what you've made me do!' ☺.

It has been said that killing girls and outwitting the law gave Bundy a sense of real achievement. The former reason I don't agree with whatsoever. The killings were to satisfy his sadistic sexual hunger. However, the satisfaction gained from outwitting law enforcement was a by-product of his most basic need – one of contempt for the 'system' and society itself. It has also been said by a few notable psychologists and psychiatrists that Bundy enjoyed the challenge of luring the smartest, most beautiful female students to their deaths. That is a somewhat sweeping statement when we know that he would often steal his way into a young woman's room, or dorm, and commit the most heinous attacks while the victim or victims slept. There is nothing smart or clever about that is there? Nor is there anything clever about the abduction, rape and murder of his final victim, twelve-year-old Lake City Junior High School girl, Kimberly Leach.

'A man who is his own lawyer has a fool for a client'.

Proverb

While in a Colorado jail awaiting trial for the murder of Caryn Campbell, Bundy contacted the celebrated attorney, Millard C. Farmer, founder of 'Team Defense', an organisation for helping convicted murderers faced with the death penalty. Farmer subsequently enjoyed a distinguished fifty-two-year civil rights career but this later all came tumbling down when, on Monday, 4 November 2019, the Supreme Court of Georgia disbarred him following a 2018 federal racketeering trial. Back in 1979, Bundy and Farmer became 'friends'. Bundy escaped the Colorado jail and it wasn't until he reached Florida and three more women had been murdered that he was arrested again. When Farmer heard that Bundy had got himself arrested again the attorney groaned: 'He's got himself arrested in the Death Belt of America, and Florida is its buckle.'

Ted Bundy imagined that he was a 'player' – a man who could run rings around the cops and the American criminal justice system. His own warped ego told him so. They always say that an empty kettle makes the loudest noise, and we can see this is true of Bundy when he was conducting his own defence. Bundy's second trial, for the murders committed at the Chi Omega sorority house, started in Miami, Florida on Monday, 25 June 1979 – His Honour, Judge Edward Douglas Cowart presiding.

Much to Ted's chagrin, Farmer was not allowed to defend him in the 'Sunshine State', for his reputation for courtroom histrionics had influenced the judge against the attorney. But, to his credit, it was Farmer who negotiated a deal with the prosecution. If Bundy would plead guilty to three murders, there would be neither a public trial nor death penalty. Initially, Bundy reluctantly agreed but, almost from the outset, Bundy made life almost impossible for his defence team because it was they who were holding centre stage, not him. He wanted to stand in the limelight and he would not tolerate being sidelined.

He decided to play for 'double or quits'. In fact, he might as well been playing Russian Roulette knowing that there were five rounds in a six-chambered revolver.

It was undoubtedly his interference in the proceedings that finally booked him a seat in Florida's three-legged 'Ol Sparky'. This, on its own, sums up Bundy's psychopathology.

It is fair to say that initially Bundy scored a very early minor success when his legal objections succeeded in having his trial moved from the state capital, Tallahassee, to Miami on the grounds that Tallahassee jurors would be prejudiced. But from then on, it was clear that he was losing ground fast. The evidence against him was overwhelming and damning. There was the witness, Nita Neary, who had seen him leave the Chi Omega sorority house on the grounds of the Florida State University campus. There was the stocking mask found in the room of Cheryl Thomas, the woman who had survived Bundy's attack on her in her home just moments after he'd left the sorority house. The mask was identical to another one found in Bundy's car. And then there were the bite marks left on Lisa Levy's left buttock, which dental experts testified matched Bundy's own teeth. This became the final nail in his coffin. He was found guilty and sentenced to death for the murders of Margaret Bowman and Lisa Levy. Bundy's trial for Carol Da Ronch's abduction and lucky escape started in Orlando on Monday, 7 January 1980. The public were vindicated when he was found guilty of killing Kimberly Leach a month later. Of interest is survivor Carol Da Ronch's story in Netflix's Ted Bundy Docuseries.

So, does Ted Bundy deserve a special place in Hell? To help us answer this question we must look to Judge Cowart (1925–1987) and his controversial sentencing remarks. Bear in mind that the judge was enormously keen in quoting from the Holy Bible when it suited him, yet here the judge encapsulates all that makes up this heinous monster in a few lines:

'The court finds that both of these killings [Lisa Levy and Margaret Bowman] were indeed heinous, atrocious and cruel. And, that they were extremely wicked, shockingly evil, vile and the product of a design to inflict a high degree of pain and utter difference to human life. The court, independent of, but in agreement with the advisory sentence rendered by the jury, does hereby impose the death penalty upon the defendant Theodore Robert Bundy. It is further ordered that on such scheduled date that you'll be put to death by a current of electricity, sufficient to cause your immediate death, and that such current of electricity shall continue to pass through your body until you are dead.

'Take care of yourself, young man [to Bundy]. I say that to you sincerely; take care of yourself. It is an utter tragedy for this court to see such a total waste of humanity, I think, as I've experienced in this courtroom.

'You're a bright young man. You'd have made a good lawyer and I would have loved to have you practise in front of me, but you went another way, partner. I don't feel any animosity toward you. I want you to know that. Take care of yourself.'

A former Miami police officer, Judge Cowart died of a heart attack aged sixty-two on 3 August 1987. Bundy was executed two years later in 1989 after failing numerous appeals to Judge Cowart and the Court of Appeals to overturn his sentence or be granted a new trial. His last visitor was his mother and her final words to him were 'You will always be my precious son.'

'Burn Bundy Burn' and 'Bundy Burgers Coming Soon'
Placard slogans outside the prison
while Bundy was being fried

All homicides are gruesome affairs. Sado-sexual homicides where the victim is subjected to extreme mental and physical torture and pain are, without doubt, heinous, wicked, cruel and inhumane. So perhaps it is by these morbid criteria we, ourselves, must judge Bundy and what we do *not* know about his murders could well be more horrific than what we actually *do* know.

With a least thirty killings under his belt – or should I say the electric chair straps – we do know that after he had secured his victims he took most of them to isolated areas where he raped and strangled them before bludgeoning them to death. Bundy would sometimes revisit their corpses repeatedly, grooming their hair, roughly applying makeup and performing sex acts with the decomposing bodies which were bloated, riddled with insects and stinking to high heaven until putrefaction and destruction by wild animals made any further interactions impossible. We also know that he decapitated twelve of his victims; keeping several of the severed heads in his apartment as 'trophies' and as macabre sexual aids forcing his penis into the agape mouths until he ejaculated. Many of his victims were not discovered until their bodies were badly decomposed and some were never found. But we know precisely how Linda Levy and Margaret Bowman met their deaths and the details of the wounds that he inflicted on these beautifully sorority sisters, so can we even begin to imagine what his other prey went through? It doesn't bear thinking about, does it? Therefore, I award this cultural super-monster Bundy a special place in Hell.

There is killing and there is 'overkilling', and this was what Peter Kürten and Ted Bundy were all about. The same dreadful homicidal criteria also applies to the now executed David Alan Gore (1953–2012). Gore was one of the 'Killing Cousins' along with his accomplice, Fred Waterfield, in Vero Beach and Indian River County, Florida. In correspondence to me, the aptly named Gore described in shocking detail how he took several young girls to his isolated barn, raped them, hung them up like a deer kill, stripped them naked, sliced their skin, bit their nipples off and inserted blunt objects into their vaginas and rectums while they screamed in immeasurable suffering. And this went on and on for hours until they breathed their last. Can one imagine what his six victims went through? Gore and Waterfield's victim count was considerably less than Bundy's but the sado-sexual drive to commit these unfathomably heinous crimes must have been similar.

***

Kenneth Alessio Bianchi and Angelo 'Tony' Buono

'Locked alone in a small cubicle with the notorious, unshackled "Hillside Strangler" it was like looking into the eyes of a Great White shark – as black as coal and unblinking and with the evil radiating from him across the table I felt his wicked tentacles of thought trying to penetrate my mind.'

The author upon meeting Kenneth Bianchi at the Washington State Penitentiary, September 1996

I met Bianchi three times. The first time I interviewed him up close and personal in a small room at the 'pen'. I met him again while he was tramping through the snow to the exercise yard. And the last time I met Bianchi was when I unexpectedly called upon him without making a prior appointment at his 'home' on the Special Housing Unit (SHU). He went ape because I had, within a few days, become his most hated nemesis, and I will tell you why.

I had been corresponding with Bianchi for several years before I met him in the flesh. I wrote to him that I believed that he might well be innocent of the crimes he'd been convicted of. I told him that, as a well-known crime writer, I was in a strong position to try and bring his protestations of innocence to the public at large. 'Think about it, Kenny,' I said. 'Think about all the TV people and media who will sit up and listen.' Being a narcissistic, ego-driven, criminal psychopath like Bundy, Ken believed my bullshit and took it in hook, line and sinker. You see that, although psychopaths are control freaks and master manipulators who thrive on controlling others including even the police and the psychiatrists who examine them, it is that very same psychopathology that *always* proves their undoing. They say that the easiest person to sell something to is another salesman – simply put: bullshit baffles brains. So, having established my bonafides to Bianchi's satisfaction, he started to send me many letters and documents and then *many more* documents and *many more* letters. This psychopath was now on my hook and all I had to do was reel him in.

Bianchi – let's call him Ken – thought I was his friend forever and a day. Buddies. Brothers-in-arms in pursuit of 'Justice for Ken'. But what never once crossed this master manipulator's mind was that it was me who was manipulating him. His over-inflated ego couldn't comprehend of such a thing happening.

I had conned Bianchi into giving me an exclusive interview and there I now was, sitting inches away from a real monster. But, for some reason, he was 'unhappy' and started staring me down. Those unblinking black eyes of his made a sudden switch to hatred. So – gulp – to break the ice, I got up from my chair, walked around to him, put my arm on his shoulder and whispered in his ear, 'C'mon, you miserable fucker, give your mate a smile.'

'God, that was a dangerous thing to do, Christopher,' I hear you say. 'Alone with that guy… he could have ripped your head off before the guards could have unlocked the door to get in.'

Well, my answer would be that I had no such fear. Because Bianchi is a paedophile child killer, a cowardly sado-sexual murderer of women and little girls. All mouth and no trousers, he is the extreme narcissist and bully that he always was. When any guy fronted him, his bottle would drop. I was right in his space, staring into his pockmarked face and the zillion micro circuits in his brain were zipping around in a confused state more-or-less reverting to their factory settings as he thought, 'Oh, shit, what do *I* do next?'

Was I not scared? I am asked many times by readers, students and guests at my lectures and talks. 'Nooo! Not at all,' I reply, with a look of absolute nonchalance. And the reason why I wasn't afraid was that I had been studying *everything* about Bianchi's life from cradle to that present day. I knew his wants, his needs, his dreams his nightmares, his aims and his fears. So I knew exactly what buttons to push, what buttons not to push to get the end result that *I* wanted. Actually, this is not rocket science; even you my dear reader can pull this off if you desperately wanted to sit up close and personal with an un-cuffed homicidal maniac – with the understanding that you may become immediately incontinent if you do manage to get out of the prison alive.

Yes, I had an hour with Ken in that room during which time I hinted that I felt that he had been disingenuous with me, somewhat economical with the truth with me – his best friend in the whole wide world forever and many days. 'But Ken... you told me that you had lost seven pages of your police statement,' I said. 'But... hey,

Ken... some officers found them in your cell during a search [which I had instigated months earlier] and now I have them... Ummm, you also told me a load of other stuff that wasn't true and I have the FBI non-secretor reports proving you have lied to me.'

I had started asking questions for which he had no answers. I was using a form of what is now known as the 'Reid Interrogation Technique' first developed in the US in the 1950s by psychologist John E. Reid, a polygraph expert and former Chicago police officer. You can see a master-class example of the Reid Technique being used on YouTube where Canadian killer Russell Williams is interrogated and eventually confesses to police. Honest to God, it's a cracker. Back in them tha old days, it was often the 'hard guy-nice guy' interrogation technique; somewhat if not downright intimidating all designed to keep a suspect off-balance. But the Reid Technique is more buddy-buddy all so carefully developed to lead the suspect up the garden path and into a sense of non-threatening security before the trap snaps shut.

My interview with Ken finished. As he was being escorted from the room by burly guards, he flipped, snarling at me, '...and don't ever, *ever* come near me again or I'll fuckin' kill you!' So, can you see that he was 'all mouth and no trousers' here. He was acting with bravado in front of the correctional officers so as not to lose face, yet as meek as a lamb when sitting down with me in that small locked cubicle. It can be great fun sometimes interviewing such pathetic scum, winding them up like a clock until their spring breaks. Great fun, even more so when there I was again, just feet away as he shuffled through the snow on his way to 'Yard Time'.

I greeted him with: 'Hi, Kenny and how is *your* day?' He looked down at his shoes and moved on without looking at me the once.

My last call with Mr Bianchi was at his 'house'. He'd previously told me in correspondence that he had the biggest, most comfortable cell in the facility – 'two cells knocked into one' he had said – to accommodate him as he being one of the most respected cons in a prison population of circa 2,000 inmates. He was a trustee, he boasted, could go more or less anywhere, whenever he so chose. He had the run of the facility he bragged. Yet he could never have envisaged in a million years that Christopher would, or even *could* be allowed by the authorities, to come a-knockin' on his front door. So, there he was, on his tiny bunk in a cell one could not swing a mouse by its tail in. He had headphones on and was listening to some music. I walked the yellow 'Do Not Cross' line down that long tier then back to cross that yellow line.

Now up close and personal – I was at his steel-barred front door – I greeted him, 'Hi, Kenny.' He didn't move an inch. Much louder this time with: 'HIIIII, Kenneth, it's your Christopher come to visit you in your BIG HOUSE, you asshole!' He flipped, as in *big time*. He flew off his bunk to his door ranting and raving, calling out and pleading for the guards to arrest me for breaching his civil rights and blah, blah, blah.

'Ya know, Kenny...' I said smiling ear-to-ear, 'I am handing all of those letters and documents you sent to me over to the authorities in your appeal. Ya'll have a nice day now and maybe a bit of paint might spruce your house up a bit cos that dirty cream colour don't suit a man of your station in life at all. Byeee!'

Oh, my, I am such a Christian-hearted soul. I almost want to burst into song with, 'What a Friend We Have in Jesus', but I won't. Nevertheless, after that, he screamed a lot of expletives at those ever so nice correctional officers, and they threw Bianchi into the hole for a month. Meanwhile, I walked out of the pen and went fishing for Steelheads in the San Juan Islands, drank cold beer in Gig Harbor and put away as much clam chowder and fresh lobster as any man could take. Well didn't I just say that interviewing monsters like Bianchi can be great fun? It gives one a great deal of delight to run rings around a homicidal psychopath as a kind of payback. Would you not agree?

But, I have digressed, as all my loyal readers will know is my wont from time to time, so let's get back to the nitty gritty and why Kenneth Alessio Bianchi and his accomplice Angelo 'Tony' Buono deserve their own 'special house' in Hell.

Bianchi was born Tuesday, 22 May 1951 in Rochester, New York. His mother was an alcoholic and a sex worker. Kenneth was quickly adopted by Frances Piccione and Nicholas Bianchi and the kid went downhill from then on.

During my research into Bianchi's past, I interviewed Frances for a radio programme and she confirmed that he was a compulsive liar. Indeed, so convincing and accomplished a liar was he that she said that even though she knew Ken was lying out of his back teeth she actually started believing him.

But we aren't going to dwell on Bianchi's childhood. Instead, I will begin with a controversy. Bianchi was tried and convicted of the Hillside Strangler murders which took place in Los Angeles, California, between October 1977 and February 1978. But Bianchi is also a suspect in another series of murders in his home city of Rochester, New York which took place between 1971 and 1973: 'The Alphabet Murders' also known as 'The Double Initial Murders'. There are two camps on this issue with around eighty-eight percent arguing that it wasn't Ken who dunnit with the remainder saying that he dunnit. I am in the latter. In fact, I believe that I am right at the forefront of the latter because when we look at his later confirmed kills do we not see the very beginnings of his MO with the earlier Rochester sex slayings? Furthermore, all three victims in that series were girls aged ten or eleven whose surnames began with the same letter as that of their first names. Each girl had been sexually assaulted and murdered by either manual or ligature strangulation before her body was discarded in or near a town or village also beginning with the same name as her initials.

'Whenever Kenneth had a big problem, or one of his girlfriends dumped him, it seems that he went out and killed someone.'

Adoptive mother, Frances Piccione,
speaking to the author

Around 4.20 p.m., Tuesday, 16 November 1971, Carmen G. Colón, a ten-year-old Puerto Rican disappeared while running an errand in Rochester for her grandmother. She had visited a chemist to collect a prescription, which wasn't as yet processed, so she told the storeowner, Jack Corbin, 'I got to go.' She left the pharmacy and was seen climbing into a dark red car, which in every respect was identical to the red Ford Pinto hatchback owned by twenty-year-old Bianchi at that time.

Some fifty minutes later, dozens of motorists driving along Interstate 490 [New York State] saw a girl answering Carmen's description, naked from the waist down, frantically waving her arms and shouting in an attempt to flag down a passing vehicle. At least one driver observed the girl being led back to a red hatchback by a man answering Bianchi's description, too.

Two days later, two teenage lads found Carmen's partially nude corpse in a gully quite close to I-490 and near to the village of Churchville some thirteen miles west of Rochester. Police discovered her coat in a culvert about 300 feet from her crumpled body. Her trousers were found on 30 November close to the service road near where the many motorists had seen her attempting to escape from a young man.

At autopsy, the medical examiner noted that Carmen had been raped. The child had also suffered a skull fracture (probably caused by her head being smashed on the rock where she lay), and one of her vertebrae had been fractured before she had been manually strangled to death. Furthermore, her body had been extensively scratched by fingernails. Carmen now rests at the Holy Sepulchre Cemetery, Rochester, Monroe County, New York. It is of some interest to know that Bianchi's adoptive mother stated that her son was often driven to violence by personal failures and that this terrible homicide took place within days of Bianchi being kicked out of his then marital home because of adultery and learning of his third set of failed exam results.

Seventeen months later, at about 5 p.m. on Monday, 2 April 1973, eleven-year-old Wanda Lee Walkowitz vanished from the east side of Rochester while returning home from an errand to buy groceries at a delicatessen. Her fully clothed body was discovered by a police officer the following day, discarded like garbage at the base of a hillside alongside an access road to State Route 104 in the town of Webster, approximately seven miles from Rochester. Somewhat ironically, Webster's town motto is: 'Where Life is Worth Living'. The position of Wanda's body indicated she had likely been thrown from a vehicle, with her corpse rolling down the embankment – a form of disposal that is repeated in many of Bianchi and Buono's later homicides. During my research, I established that this murder coincided almost to the day that Bianchi – now the owner of a light-tan Dodge Dart – was thrown out of his then girlfriend's apartment. Janice Tuschong, his girlfriend, had caught him sleeping with a woman called Donna Duranso.

At autopsy, it was revealed Wanda had been raped, then strangled from behind with a ligature, most likely a belt. Several defensive wounds indicated that she had fought with her killer. Her body had been redressed after death. Revealed also were traces of semen and pubic hair upon the victim. Of significance to us is that several strands of white cat fur were found upon her clothing. The Walkowitz family didn't own a white cat but Frances Piccione did. In her interview with me she explained that quite often the cat would find its way into Kenneth's Dodge Dart. But of even more significance, the semen traces found on Wanda's body were from a non-secretor – a person whose saliva and other secretions, including semen, do not contain blood-group antigens. Eighty-five percent of the population are secretors, so non-secretors are in a minority. Bianchi always maintained, swore black and blue, that he was a secretor, when he in fact is *most definitely* not!

Police enquiries produced an eyewitness who told investigators that he'd observed Wanda standing alongside the passenger door of a large brown vehicle talking to the driver. This witness was unable to obtain a clear view of the occupant, although the location of this sighting was just a fifth of a mile from the girl's home. However, another witness had observed a man forcing a red-haired girl matching Wanda's description into a light-coloured or tan Dodge Dart on Conkey Avenue between 5.30 p.m. and 6 p.m. on the evening of her disappearance. Wanda is buried in the same cemetery as Carmen Colón.

Bianchi's affair with Donna Duranso collapsed in November 1973 and, a day later, the Monday after Thanksgiving recess, another youngster vanished. During the evening of 26 November 1973, eleven-year-old Michelle Maenza was reported as missing by her mother, Carolyn, after she failed to return home from school. Subsequent investigations would determine that she was last seen by some of her classmates at approximately 3.20 p.m. walking alone enroute to a shopping plaza near to her school with the intention of retrieving a purse her mother had left inside one of the stores earlier that day. About ten minutes later, another witness saw Michelle sitting in the passenger seat of a large 'light beige' or 'tan' car travelling at high speed on Ackerman Street before turning onto Webster Avenue. According to this witness, the girl was crying.

Later that day at 5.30 p.m., a motorist saw a man standing by a large light beige or tan car with a flat tyre, parked alongside Route 350 in the town of Walworth, and he was holding a girl, who matched Michelle's description, by the wrist. When this Good Samaritan stopped to offer assistance, the man had 'grabbed the girl and pushed her behind his back' as well as trying to obscure his licence plate from the motorist's view. He stared at the motorist with such a menacing expression on his face that the witness felt compelled to drive away. This motorist was to later give police a description of this man, which, incidentally, was as close to that of Bianchi as one might get.

Michelle's fully clothed body was discovered at 10.30 a.m., on Wednesday, 28 November, lying face down in a ditch alongside a rural road in Macedon, approximately fifteen miles southeast of Rochester. Her autopsy revealed that in addition to receiving extensive blunt force trauma to her body, she had been raped, then strangled to death from behind with a ligature, possibly a thin rope. Numerous strands of white cat fur were discovered upon her clothing, and leaf samples matching the foliage where her body was discovered were recovered from within one of her clenched hands, indicating she had likely been strangled to death at, or near to, the location where she was found. Detectives were able to retrieve a partial palm print from her neck and traces of semen which were later determined to have come from a non-secretor.

An analysis of the contents of Michelle's stomach revealed traces of a hamburger and onions which had been eaten approximately one hour before her murder, giving credence to earlier reports of a girl matching her description having been seen in the company of a Caucasian male with dark hair, aged between twenty-five and thirty-five, approximately six feet tall and weighing 165 pounds, both seen at a fast food restaurant in the town of Penfield at approximately 4.30 p.m. on the afternoon of her disappearance, and alongside Route 350 about one hour later.

As with most homicide cases there were several suspects who seemed to fit the bill, however I have been reliably informed by the Rochester Police Department, that all of them, with the exception of Bianchi, have been ruled out. So before we move on to the Hillside Strangler killings, it is worth remembering these unsolved cases. All three girls had been raped then strangled to death, a similar MO to Bianchi's Los Angeles murders. There were other parallels too. All three girls lived in rundown neighbourhoods. All were walking alone when they were taken away. All were from broken homes – their fathers gone, the mothers on welfare. All had eaten a small meal just before they met with their deaths. There was the white cat fur attached to their clothing. Each girl was last seen alive in the company of a white male who pretty much matched Bianchi's description at that time. And there are the similarities between the cars described by witnesses and the vehicles that Bianchi was driving at the time. Indeed, it is interesting to note that Bianchi made a revealing slip of the tongue during my interview with him. He had asked what sort of car I was driving back in the UK. I told him that it was a 'Signal Red' 5.3 litre Jaguar XJS. He threw it back replying, 'I had a red hatchback when I was much younger... it seems that we both like the colour of blood.'

All three girls were also streetwise. They had been warned by their mothers not to talk to strangers, so investigators reasoned that whoever had abducted them might have posed as a police officer, a clergyman or some other trusted figure of authority. This sort of masquerade fits hand-in-glove with Bianchi's later methods of entrapping victims. In Los Angeles he and Buono would be undercover cops using a fake cop shield bought at a 'swap-meet' to convince women that they were under arrest or otherwise in trouble. He had once tried to steal someone's identity in order to pose as a genuine psychologist to lure young women to a room he rented from a real shrink. Later, in Bellingham, Washington State, he cast himself as a 'Captain Bianchi', when he was nothing more than a menial security guard working for the Whatcom Security Agency (WSA). He used this position there to convince co-eds Karan Mandic and Diane Wilder to take a house-sitting job thereby giving him the opportunity to attack and kill them both. Indeed, even to this very day in prison, he frequently reinvents himself. He's adopted the shiny, new, squeaky clean Italian names: 'Nicholas Fontana' and 'Anthony D'Amato'. He's even dubbed himself the Reverend K. Bianchi, claiming that he is one of the world's leading experts on religions. He wrote in a letter to me to explain:

'I have academically completed a Ministerial training programme given by the Evangelical Theological Seminary, and I am blessed to have been ordained by a Full Gospel Church back in 1986. My faith has taken me on an exploratory course. I have even mailed out, free of charge, a written homily entitled *Word on the Word*. I ceased doing it because it became too expensive. I would not, and cannot, accept donations.'

Speaking to an assistant warden, I learned that he had raked in as much cash as he could before the Washington Department of Corrections stopped him from running his own 'Save Kenneth Bianchi Campaign'. It also transpires that for years, Bianchi's church (one of several he has co-opted) had sent Reverent K. Bianchi quarterly newsletters detailing forthcoming religious events. This, you will be pleased to learn, didn't last because when James Blodgett, a new, tough, no-nonsense prison administrator took over, Bianchi's ordination certificate and letters were confiscated. So, suck on that Kenny m'lad!

Bianchi has claimed he has multiple personality disorders and has faked hypnosis. He has even fooled several of America's leading psychiatrists. At one time he pretended that he had terminal cancer to gain sympathy from his common-law wife. He sells sketches he claims are drawn by him, citing his 'Associate in Arts Degree' that he received in June 1988. In fact, he cannot draw a straight line using a ruler and the sketches are the artwork of inmates *who can actually draw*. Bianchi simply signs them off with his name. And, to top it all, he claims that he is a Member of the American Bar Association and has a 'Juris Doctor Degree'. Can we not see this pathological 'Billy Liar', as his mother called him, easily enticing three vulnerable little girls into his car? Of course we can. And can we call him a murderous Pinocchio? Yes. Why not?

It goes without saying that Bianchi was and still is in the frame for the 'Alphabet Murders' but during his only interview with Rochester homicide cops he was as plausible as ever. A natural-born liar – well able to sell ice cream to Eskimos and spectacles to the totally blind – he convinced investigators that he had watertight alibis for the three murders in question. However, he refused – as was his legal right in those days – to give body fluid samples, which would have confirmed that he was a non-secretor. So, suspicion fell away. Not one police officer checked to confirm the veracity of Ken's alibis. The reason given was that there were stronger links to other suspects at the time – all of whom later proved inconsequential in the grand scheme of things. What, however, does gall me is this: ever so anxious to clean up the slate on these three child homicides, the police at the time laid into one man and labelled him the chief suspect – after he had conveniently committed suicide that is and due to the stress of being wrong accused and hounded.

And what *might* have happened if Bianchi's alibis *had* been checked out? During the course of carrying out research for a book chapter on Bianchi and a TV documentary, I spoke to the providers of the alibis in question, including Janice Tuschong. And I learned that Ken's claims were not worth the paper they were written on. This poses some intriguing questions. Why would he fabricate alibis if he had nothing to hide? Why would he refuse to give body fluid samples if he had nothing to fear? Why he did he deny, then later admit to me (of course, *only* after I told him that I had it confirmed) that his mother *did* own a white cat?

Bianchi vehemently claims that he has been ruled out as a suspect in these three Rochester murders, but this is *not* the case at all. When I visited Rochester PD, I met with the now retired Captain Lynde Johnston on matters concerning the serial killer, Arthur John Shawcross. Captain Johnston has a fascination with Jack the Ripper and he had already read one of my books. He told me that Bianchi had always been in the frame, and there were no ifs and buts about it. So this leaves us with a whodunit to solve. Bianchi has always claimed to be a secretor. He says that he could never have been involved in any of the rapes, torturing and slayings he has been convicted of, in a meek 'Nah, not me, guv!' sort of way. Indeed, he went as far as stating, in countless letters to me, that he could produce his medical notes to prove this claim. However, when pressed to supply these documents at interview, Bianchi avoided the subject before admitting, 'Actually, I am not sure if I am a secretor, or non-secretor. I just don't know, Chris.'

To assist Kenneth on this issue, and in my search for the facts, I contacted the FBI. They released a document dated Wednesday, 2 June 1982. In it, Agent Robert Beams, a specialist in blood grouping and body fluids, confirmed that, after taking samples from Bianchi, he was able to categorically say that Bianchi *was* a non-secretor. More to the point, the cell search I instigated at the prison revealed that Bianchi had had a copy of that FBI document, and it had been in his possession for a long time. Quite obviously Ken believes that everyone in this world is a mug, except himself.

So, now is the time to move on very quickly to Los Angeles – 'The City of Angels' – way down south in

'The Golden State' of California. The year is 1975 and Bianchi, carrying all his meagre worldly possessions, alighted from a bus at the Eagle Plaza stop in Glendale. Here, he is to be greeted by his half cousin, Angelo 'Tony' Buono who is Frances Piccione's nephew – or something along those lines. To be honest with you, we cannot be quite a hundred per cent sure. But what we *can* be sure about are the dreadful murders that followed this fateful meeting.

For a while, Bianchi and Buono made money by forcing young women into sex work and acting as their pimps. Two girls, Sabra Hannan and Becky Spears managed to escape them. They tried to purchase a 'trick list' from local sex worker Deborah Noble and her friend Yolanda Washington. Yolanda was the first victim in the Hillside Strangling series.

At 1.34 p.m. on Monday, 18 October 1977, Yolanda's naked body was found sprawled on its stomach alongside Forest Lawn Drive; close to the famous cemetery of the same name and just south of the Ventura Freeway. Crime scene photos show her right hand crooked over, her legs apart. It appeared that she had been dragged from a vehicle and dropped near a pile of broken road-surfacing concrete. Behind the corpse was a yellow 'NO TRESPASSING OR LOITERING' sign. A tall and striking black woman, Yolanda was immediately identified by vice officers. She was a particularly attractive nineteen-year-old, who had almond-shaped eyes and medium-length black hair, she was a part-time waitress and sex worker who was known to have touted for business with Deborah Noble. Enquiries soon established that she was last seen alive just before midnight as she solicited for business at Vista and Sunset Boulevards. On a good night, she could earn over US$300, which helped her support her two-year-old daughter, Tameika. The autopsy showed that she'd had sex with two men shortly before death – one of whom was a non-secretor. She had been strangled with a piece of cloth while she was lying down. There were marks around her wrists. She had been raped anally too.

Bianchi told me that he had killed her in the back seat of his car and had removed a turquoise ring from her finger, which he gave to his common-law wife, Kelli Kae Boyd. This ring was found in Kelli's possession when Bianchi was finally arrested in Bellingham, Washington State, in 1979.

Bianchi later told police that Yolanda was not the stranglers' first kill. When the Hillside Strangler task force was assembled in December 1977, Laura Collins' name was erased from the victims list. It was not until January 1978 that the then Assistant Chief of Police, Darryl Gates, publicly indicated that Laura was indeed a victim of the Hillside Stranglers. Laura Collins, twenty-two years old, was last seen alive just after noon at Ventura Freeway and Lankershim Boulevard, on Sunday, 4 September 1977. Her partially clothed body was found near the Forest Lawn exit slip road off the Ventura Freeway, Burbank, at 10.30 a.m. on Friday, 9 September. She had been strangled. This homicide became more-or-less the blueprint for all of the subsequent killings.

Judith 'Judy' Ann Miller, a fifteen-year-old white female, was abducted from the Hollywood area of Howard and Wilcox just after midnight on Monday,

31 October 1977. An unassuming girl, with medium-length reddish-brown hair, Judy lived in a ramshackle hotel which was her base as a part-time sex worker. She was from trailer-park stock. Her mother was wanted in connection with welfare fraud. Her father had jumped bail for a similar offence.

It was a pretty grim sight that Halloween morning at Alta Terrace and La Crescenta. Judy's naked body lay close to the kerb in a middle-class residential area. Her body had been covered with a tarpaulin by a nearby property owner to shield the corpse from the neighbourhood children. The bruises around her neck showed that she had been strangled. She had ligature marks on both wrists and her ankles. Insects had begun to feast on her pale skin. On one eyelid was a small piece of light-coloured fluff that Sergeant Frank Salerno of the LA County Sheriff's Department saved for the forensic experts. It did not appear that she had been strangled at this location.

The medical examiner determined that Judy had died circa midnight, some six hours before she was found. It was also clear that she had been vaginally raped and sodomised. In his police interviews, Bianchi explained that Judy had been taken back to Buono's place in Glendale where she had been raped, and that it was he who had sodomised her then strangled her. The two men then finished her off by suffocating the teenager with a plastic supermarket bag. 'She involuntarily urinated after death, just as Washington had done,' Bianchi claimed, with an evil grin playing across his mouth. 'We made her go into the washroom before we killed her to stop it happening, but it didn't work. She was tied by the arms, legs and neck to our special chair in Angelo's bedroom. She didn't like dying one bit.' These two monsters had already earned themselves a special place in Hell, don't you agree? But the truth was that they had barely even started.

Teresa or 'Lissa' Kastin became the stranglers' fourth victim. Aged twenty-one, she worked as a waitress at the Healthfair Restaurant near Hollywood Boulevard and Vine Street. She was stopped at 9.15 p.m. on Saturday, 5 November 1977, by Bianchi and Buono, who were posing as undercover police officers. They ordered her into their black-over-white sedan and drove her to Buono's home for what Bianchi said would be 'questioning'. There, she was tied down onto their special chair, and her striped sweater and short skirt were cut off with scissors. The two were repelled because she had hairy legs, so Bianchi raped her with a root beer bottle as he throttled her. When she kicked out in her death throes, Buono sat on her legs, shouting, 'Die, you cunt, die.' Lissa was allowed to suck in lungfuls of air many times before she lost consciousness for the last time.

At 1.15 a.m. the next day, Lissa's body was found at Linda Vista Terrace. She was identified swiftly after news broadcasts reported the murder and Lissa's father telephoned the police reporting his daughter as missing. At autopsy, no semen was present in the vagina or anus, which supported Bianchi's confession that neither of the two men had physically raped this victim. There was no suggestion that Lissa was a prostitute.

Jill Barcombe was an eighteen-year-old, white sex worker who'd moved to Hollywood following a string of convictions in New York. She was last seen alive at

Pico Boulevard and Ocean Park Boulevard at around 7.00 p.m. on Wednesday, 9 November 1977. Her body was found naked and strangled at around 5.50 a.m. the following morning at Franklin Canyon Drive and Mulholland Drive. Jill had put up a fierce fight for her life as severe head trauma was present.

Evelyn Jane King, aged twenty-eight, was an aspiring actress and part-time model with real 'wow factor'. She was rated by the 'Hollywood Set' and had exploded on the scene when she was just sixteen. She was also a Scientology student and a follower of L. Ron Hubbard. Police at the time suggested that she was involved in sex work, although this was totally incorrect.

Jane (she liked that better than Evelyn) was last seen alive in a quiet, residential area outside 9500 Lemona Avenue, at 10.10 p.m. on Wednesday, 9 November. Again posing as undercover vice cops, Bianchi and Buono 'arrested' her on suspicion of prostitution and took her back to Buono's place where she was dragged screaming through into the east bedroom where she was stripped naked. Bianchi confessed that they were delighted to find her pubis was shaven. However, because she struggled while she was being raped, the two monsters decided to teach her a lesson. A plastic bag was placed over her head while Bianchi sodomised her. Jane pleaded desperately for her life during a four-hour period of abject terror before she was allowed to suffocate to death as Bianchi climaxed.

Jane's badly decomposing body was found on a bed of dead leaves in undergrowth at the Los Feliz exit off-ramp of the Golden State Freeway on Wednesday, 23 November. She lay on her back, legs open, with the right knee drawn up. Insects had already started to feast on her body. What a tragic end to what could have been a wonderful life? Her two killers must be almost subhuman and scum of the worst kind. But, the double murder of Sonja Marie Johnson (fourteen) and Dolores 'Dolly' Ann Cepeda (twelve), shocked everyone involved in the case because of the violence and brutality. Judge Roger Boren, former prosecutor at Bianchi and Buono's trial, told me, years later, at his LA home:

> 'Buono and Bianchi followed the girls on a bus as they travelled from the Eagle Rock Plaza mall in Glendale, and apparently used some police ruse that they were being arrested on suspicion of shoplifting. They took these two young girls to Buono's home and did with them what they did with the other victims – raped, tortured and strangled them to death. They then took the girls to a hillside overlooking one of the largest freeways in Los Angeles and discarded their bodies. That particular hillside was used by many to discard trash. There were couches, mattresses... things of that sort had been thrown down that hillside. And these two bodies had been discarded in a like manner. In fact, they were not discovered for two weeks.'

Both girls were pupils at the Saint Ignatius School, 6025 Monte Vista Street, Los Angeles. The girls were last seen alive on Sunday, 13 November 1977, boarding a bus at the Eagle Plaza stop, which was just a quarter-of-a-mile from Buono's home and car upholstery refurbishing business (since demolished) off East Colorado Street, Glendale. Once at the property, Sonja was raped and murdered in a bedroom by Buono, while Dolly sat outside with Bianchi.

'Where's my friend?' asked Dolly when Buono came out alone.

'Oh, don't worry,' said Bianchi, 'you'll be seeing her in a minute.'

The last thing Dolly saw was the face of her dead friend on the bed beside her as Bianchi raped, sodomised then strangled her. All the while she was calling out for her mom to come and save her.

Children playing on the rubbish tip at Landa Street (a thirty-five-minute drive from Buono's home) found the two girls' naked corpses at 4.00 p.m. on Sunday, 20 November. The crime scene photographs show Dolly and Sonja sprawled out among the discarded beer bottles, tin cans and piles of other trash. Visible also is a sign reading: 'NO TRASH DUMPING'. Sonja rests almost on her right side, her left hand tucked up under her breasts, her hand nudging her chin. The right arm, hand still gripped tight in a cadaveric spasm, is outstretched and underneath her right side. The position of Sonja's right hand records exactly the last physical movement she made before death supervened. Such contraction/instant rigidity persists into the period of rigor mortis – the stiffening of the body that usually appears within two to six hours after death. By the time she was dumped in Landa Street, rigor mortis was present and only dissipated later. Her legs are almost straight, the left foot draped over the neck of Dolly who is on her stomach; her torso slightly crooked and leaning to the right of her legs, which are parted. Dolly's left arm is also tucked underneath her body, her hand covering her mouth. As with Sonja, this would have been her last movement made before death and she was likely stifling screams as Bianchi killed her. When one sees such horrendous things, only then can we start to understand the true, evil nature of Bianchi and Buono. The right arm, bent at the elbow, was outstretched. Human bite marks were evident on her left buttock. The position of the bodies tells us that the girls were dragged one at a time headfirst from a car and up into the garbage dump. In Bianchi's confession, he revealed that, after killing the two girls, they left the bodies on Buono's bed while the two men had argued about how to dispose of them.

During the course of making a television documentary on The Hillside Stranglers, I visited the site on Landa Street with former LAPD homicide detective, Leroy Orozco. It was starting to rain as we tramped up a narrow path, my film crew trailing behind us. To the east is West Silver Lake Drive, the busy freeway Roger Boren mentioned, then the massive Silver Lake Reservoir. In the distant grey haze the towering buildings of Los Angeles.

'The public was just outraged that we, law enforcement officers, could not do anything to stop these brutal murders. Especially the single women in this city who went to work at nights, going to the markets, going to see their families. They were petrified.'

Homicide Detective Richard Crotsley,
LAPD to the author at interview

Sonja Johnson (1963–1977) is buried at the Resurrection Cemetery, Montebello LA. Dolores 'Dolly' Ann Cepeda (1964–1977) is buried in the Forest Lawn Memorial Park, Glendale, LA.

Kathleen 'Kathy' Kimberly Robinson was another attractive girl, well known around the hotspots of Hollywood. Aged seventeen, her flowing blonde hair caught the attention of the Hillside Stranglers at 9.30 p.m. on Wednesday, 16 November 1977. She was walking towards her car parked near Pico Boulevard and Ocean Boulevard, when Buono and Bianchi drew up alongside her. Flashing the phony police badge, they ordered her into their car. She was found fully clothed, strangled, with her throat cut, at South Burnside Avenue, at 8.30 a.m. the next day. Kathleen is buried at the Forest Lawn Memorial Park, Cypress, Orange County CA.

Kristina Weckler was a twenty-year-old honours student at the Pasadena Art Center of Design in Pasadena. She lived at Tamarind Apartments on East Garfield Avenue in Glendale, and six blocks south of Buono's place on East Colorado Street. This was the same apartment complex where Bianchi had once resided, so he knew the young woman and had pestered her for a date. Kristina, who knew that Bianchi was then living with his, now pregnant, common-law wife, Kelli Boyd, had rejected his advances. Kristina's naked body was found on Ranons Avenue on Sunday, 20 November. Detective Sergeant Bob Grogan immediately noticed the ligature marks on her wrists, ankles and neck. When he turned the body over, blood oozed from her rectum. The bruises on her breasts were obvious. Oddly, there were two puncture marks on her arm, but no signs of the needle tracks that would indicate drug addiction.

Bianchi later told police that around 6.00 p.m. on Saturday, 19 November, he had knocked on Kristina's door and flashed his phony shield, telling her that he was now a police officer. He said that someone had crashed into her car which was parked outside in the road. Once outside the safety of her apartment she was bundled into his car and driven to Buono's home. But this time they tried to kill her using a new method. They injected Kristina with caustic cleaning fluid. What follows is Bianchi's statement to the police. Verbatim, it makes for shocking reading:

'He [Buono] suggested that ... he said, "How about just injecting air into her? The air bubble would probably kill her." I said, "Oh, you want to try something different then. Whatever."

'We both walked back into the dining room, put the chair back at the dining room table. He grabbed her underwear and her socks and he went back into the room and set the needle down on the bed ... at one end of the bed and he said to her, "Come on, now, we're going to stand up." And we both helped her up.

'He said, "Sit down here," and she sat on the edge of the bed and he helped her get her clothes on, her underwear and socks. He said, "OK, now come on. Stand up." And he helped her stand up and we walked her to the open part of the room at the bottom of the bed and set her down on the floor, face up. He took the needle, took the cap off of it, he pulled back the plunger and he told me, he said, "Hold her legs." I held her legs. He crouched down. He's on her left side. He stuck the needle in her neck [left side] and pushed the plunger in and pulled it out.

'He did it a couple of times. She flinched and made a murmuring sound and he stood up and he said, "Let go of her legs." And he walked towards me and pushed me lightly back towards the doorway and he says, "Just stand here and see what happens." So I stood there for about five to ten minutes. Nothing happened. He says, "What I should do is put something in the needle. Stay here. I'll be right back." He went into the kitchen area. When he came back there was a blue solution, some kind of blue solution, in the needle.

'He injected her and said, "Help me to get her up." We helped her to her feet and she was still shaking. Walked her into the kitchen and walked her into the front where his stove was being taken out, or the connection was, and lied her down on the floor. He stood up and started to walk away from her and he indicated to me to walk away with him. He had to talk to me. We walked into the dining room, and in the dining room he said, "What I'll do is put a bag over her head," he says, "I'll use twine; I'll cut off a piece of twine, so we can make a seal on the bag," he says, "and the pipe, the bendable pipe is long enough," he says, "stick that under the bag and when I tell you, turn the gas on and when I tell you, turn the gas off."

'After we'd had a little discussion in the dining room, we walked back into the kitchen. Kristina Weckler's lying on the floor in this direction [indicating], in front of the fixture. Angelo is standing here to her left side [indicating]. She's still shaking really bad, probably from that blue stuff that was injected into her. He put the bag over her head and there was no unusual movement when he did that. He told me to get the pipe and stick the pipe under the bag, which I did. He then wrapped the twine a couple of times around her neck and pulled it tight and said, "OK, go ahead. Turn it on." I turned on the gas, the bag inflated. He said, "Turn off the gas." I turned off the gas, and he waited until it deflated. Turned it on again. We repeated this probably four or five times.

'Finally, it was obvious that she had stopped breathing, so he said to take the tubing out, which I did ... put the tubing back and made sure the valve was turned off all the way. He took the twine off of her and the bag off of her head. He took out his keys and rolled her over and I held her shoulders while he rolled her over and unlocked the handcuffs. I took off the tape and gag from her mouth and took the blindfold off and he removed her pants and underwear. We both walked into the dining room and put everything into a paper bag. He then got the roll of tape and taped up the bag. I walked to the back door. He walked to the dumpster. Moved a few things around and tossed the bag in there. Put things on top of the bag. He came back in, asked me for the keys to my car. He said, "I'll open the trunk." When he got through opening the trunk, he walked to the street, looked around and came back again... then we dumped her off.'

When the barbaric injection failed to kill her, they had covered her head with a plastic bag and piped coal gas into her lungs. Finally Bianchi raped Kristina, ejaculating into her during the moment she convulsed in death. She died as the result of strangulation by ligature.

Redheaded student and trainee secretary, eighteen-year-old Lauren Rae Wagner, disappeared on Sunday, 27 November 1977. Her father found her car parked with the driver's door open and the interior light on just across from their house and directly in front of the home of an elderly lady called Beulah Stofer. Mrs Stofer would soon tell detectives how she had seen the young woman abducted by two men. They were driving a black-over-white sedan, which she at first took to be a police car.

At 7.30 a.m. the following day, a driver on his way to work found Lauren's naked body at 1200 Cliff Drive in the Mount Washington area. Lauren was lying on her back, her left arm outstretched, her left lower leg just touching the road. Her mass of rich, red hair framed her pretty face, and her eyes were peacefully closed. Strangely, it looked as though she had burns on her palms. Like the unusual puncture marks in Kristina Weckler's arms, it looked as though the killers were experimenting – possibly with methods of torture. There was something else different – a shiny track of some sticky liquid had attracted a convoy of ants. If this substance was saliva, or semen, there was the possibility that the killer's blood type could be determined. Tests on semen found on earlier victims had revealed not much at all.

Bianchi later told police that, back at Buono's house, Lauren pretended to enjoy being raped in the desperate hope that her attackers would allow her to live. They had tried to electrocute her by attaching live wires to the palms of her hands, but this only caused extreme pain and superficial burns. Bianchi then raped her as Buono strangled her to death with a ligature.

On Monday, 14 December 1977, police were called to a vacant lot on a steep slope at 2006 N. Alvarado Street. They arrived at 7.03 a.m. The sun had just come up, and it was a clear morning with very few clouds in the sky. Rampart Divisional Patrol Unit 2-A-47 officers had responded to a radio call alerting them to a dead body lying by the road, which ran through the floor of the canyon splitting Lakeshore Drive and Alvarado Street.

When homicide detectives Oakes and Richard Crotsley arrived, they noticed that the tall, blonde victim was lying on her back in the now familiar spread-eagle position. Postmortem lividity was starting to form in her toes. The young woman was Caucasian and in her twenties. There were ligature marks around her wrists, ankles and her neck. On her left forearm she had a tattoo – a square 'cross' with four dots within its border. On the right ankle was a second tattoo of faint design bearing the name 'Kim'. With no other identification to be found, she was labelled as 'Jane Doe #112', and the strangler's penultimate Los Angeles victim was on her way to the morgue.

Using documents provided exclusively to me by the LAPD, it has since been possible to plot the victim's last hours in some detail. She was Kimberly 'Kim' aka 'Donna' Diane Martin who freelanced as an escort for 'Climax Nude Modelling', 1815 N. Serrano Avenue. At precisely 8.30 p.m. on Tuesday, 13 December, Bianchi phoned this outfit from a kiosk inside the Hollywood Library in North Ivar Street. Michelle Elaine Rodriguez took the call from a man calling himself 'Mike Ryan'. After establishing the price of $40 for a 'modelling service', 'Mike Ryan' told Rodriguez that his wife 'has left town for the first time in two years, so I would like you to send me a pretty blonde model if you could. Possibly wearing black stockings and a dress.'

After verifying that this was no prank call and calling 'Mike Ryan' back to check that he was who he allegedly said he was, Michelle Rodriguez phoned Kimberly Martin. This is part of the transcript of that call:

> Rodriguez: I have a call. It's a cash call out in Hollywood in an apartment. Do you want it?
> Kimberly: Yeah, give me the information.
> Rodriguez: Michael Ryan. Phone number 462-9794. 1950 Tamarind, Hollywood. Cash. Apartment 114. Sounds like a good call to me.

It's an apartment. It's near your location, but always be careful and make sure he's not a cop.

Kimberly: Sounds good to me. I'll give him a call.

Rodriguez: Phone me and let me know whether you'll go on it?

Kimberly: OK. Goodbye.

Kimberly Martin called her prospective client and then she rang the agency back to say that she was accepting the job. The distance from the library on Ivar Street to 1950 N. Tamarind Avenue is nearly a mile, taking an average of five minutes to drive. It transpired that Bianchi was seen sitting on the library steps by a witness at around 9 p.m. then he suddenly stood up and walked off. Buono was picking him up.

At around 9.05 p.m. Kimberly left her own apartment and drove to Tamarind, where she parked-up and walked into the lobby. Several people saw her at 9.25 p.m. Shortly thereafter, residents heard a woman screaming, 'Please don't kill me,' but all of them put it down to a domestic dispute. Minutes later, though, they found the contents of a woman's handbag strewn along the hallway.

Bianchi claims that he and Buono dragged Kimberly out through a rear entrance and into the underground car park where they'd left their car. They drove her to Buono's place, where she was tortured, raped and murdered. 'We killed her because she was fuckin' useless in bed,' Bianchi explained to detectives.

It goes without saying that prostitution is a very dangerous business at the best of times. It is also fair to say that Michelle Rodriguez at 'Climax Nude Modelling' did carry out several checks on the veracity of 'Michael Ryan's' call. Bianchi had once lived at this North Tamarind address. Kimberly would have been well aware that two highly dangerous killers were targeting women and bringing terror to Los Angeles. Indeed, police had even advised anyone that if women felt at all suspicious about a 'cop-stop', they should tell the officers to follow them to the nearest police station – a place of complete safety. As for the residents of the Tamarind apartment complex – well, what more can I say?

On Friday, 17 February 1978, the crew of an Angeles National Forest helicopter spotted an orange Datsun car, which was parked precariously close to a ravine by the Angeles Crest Highway. Thirty feet further down the incline police found a naked body. The young woman's arms were by her side, her legs apart. This was twenty-year-old Cindy Lee Hudspeth, a brunette who worked as a telephonist and was also employed as a part-time waitress at the Robin Hood Inn, a restaurant frequented by the weedy, stuttering, ferret-faced Angelo Buono who was known locally as 'The Italian Stallion'. The inn was in Burbank Blvd, Sherman Oaks – a seventeen-minute drive from his home in Glendale.

Exactly how Cindy ended up almost over the edge of a ravine was not known for some years but we now know roughly what happened to her. Buono learned from Cindy that she needed some upholstery work done on her Datsun. It is fair to say that Buono knew his stuff for he had re-upholstered many upscale motors in his time, even one driven by Frank Sinatra. Bianchi said in his statement to police that, when he turned up at Buono's auto-upholstery shop he saw Cindy's car parked outside. 'She had called to see Buono about fitting new mats for her,' he said. The two men forced Cindy onto a bed, hog-tied her, then raped and strangled her. The ordeal lasted almost two hours. Then, with her dead body in the trunk of the Datsun, Bianchi drove her car, closely followed by Buono in his sedan to the ravine. They opened the trunk and dragged the poor girl's body down the slope then tried to push the Datsun over the edge. It rolled some fifty feet then stopped but, by then, the killers had fled.

The relationship between the two men had become fraught and the time for this murderous tag-team to part company had come. Buono had become sick and tired of his sponging half-cousin who didn't have a meaningful job while he ran a successful car upholstery business. Things came to a head when Bianchi boasted that he had applied to become a police officer and was enjoying 'ride-alongs' in cop cars. Buono flipped, brandishing a pistol he kicked Bianchi out, warning him that if he ever saw him again he would blow his 'F-ff-fuckin' head off,' and he meant it too. Bianchi packed what few belongings he had, boarded a bus and rode 1,237 miles north to Bellingham, Washington State, where he moved in with his estranged common-law wife, Kellie Kae Boyd, who sick and tired of his lies had left him way back in LA. In his wake he left thirteen dead bodies, countless broken lives and a mountain of debt. But did the killing stop – no it didn't. The monster that was Bianchi would kill again. Twice.

★

'Well … Mr Bianchi? He was … a wannabe cop. He wanted
to be a police officer. He tried in his hometown of Rochester
to be a reserve. He moved to California, got involved down
there, wanted to be a deputy police officer in Los Angeles. He
actually got into their ride-along programme.
'Because of his ability to con, he talked a security agency into
thinking that he was really hot stuff, so they gave him a job in
their organisation. He became friends with several Bellingham
police officers, and he took the test, the examination for the
Bellingham Police Department.'

Crime scene officer Robert Knudsen,
Bellingham PD to the author during an interview

I like Bellingham. The small seaport city with its
population of about 60,000, sits twenty miles due south
of the Canadian border, on the northwest corner of
Washington State. It appeals to me because it is the
gateway to the Mount Baker recreational area, which
looks over one of the most magnificent vistas in the
locality – the pine-clad slopes of San Juan, the Vancouver
Islands and the Strait of Juan de Fuca.

From Los Angeles, the most straightforward route
to Bellingham is north along Interstate 5 (I-5), but in
my rental Mitsubishi Shogun me and my film producer,
Frazer Ashford, opted for the scenic route along Highway
101. In places, especially at Eureka up to Crescent City,
the road literally clings to the cliff tops with the threat
of falling boulders all adding to the excitement of the
drive alongside a drop into the raging surf of the Pacific
far below. And it was someplace along this route that we
opted for an 'Indian Breakfast'. So, please allow me to
digress for a moment or two.

We were passing through some kind of place where abandoned rusty cars and suspicious locals seemed to be everywhere – the sort of place that would not be out of place in *The Twilight Zone* – when we spotted a shed. It was a sort of down-market burger/kebab arrangement perched on wheels with no tyres. On it hung a sign: 'INDIAN BREAKFASTS HERE. FILL YA'LL BELLY FOR FIFTY CENTS' – or something like that. So we pulled over in a cloud of dust, and hauled our numbed backsides out of our vee-hicle, as ya'll do, and we ordered two Indian Breakfasts. Now, we weren't quite sure what the edible constituents of such a repast would be. The meal preparation began with 'chef' throwing a ball of dough – no bigger than a human testicle – mixed with something else into a pan of boiling hot oil. I was rather peckish so I ordered two balls and Frazer did the same. And then we started munching these two balls of fried greasy something.

'Did you move my seat forward?' asked Frazer. 'No,' I replied, while noting that my own seat seemed to have moved. 'But the steering wheel is getting closer to my stomach. Look,' he groaned. If one has ever eaten an 'Indian Breakfast' – most likely a native American food – one will know that one is eating something resembling food that, once swallowed, expands to about fifty-plus times its original size. And we, being plum dumb stupid had – against chef's advice – each eaten two of them. The pain, the agony, the bloating... oh fuckkkk! I'm not sure if it was the invention of the Chippewa, Apache, Sioux, or the Cheyenne but, whoever invented it, had the intention of not just filling one's belly for fifty cents but making sure it was full for a week or more.

So, back to Bianchi who was now residing in Bellingham, WA and had moved in with his common-law wife, Kellie. Bianchi started working as a security guard at a Fred Myer superstore out on Interstate 5. He duly repaid his employer by stealing all manner of brand new tools – which were later found in the basement of Kellie's home. It was whilst working at Fred Myer, that he met a very pretty Washington State University co-ed. Twenty-two years old, with long blonde hair, Karen Mandic worked part-time as a cashier. He pestered her for a date but she already had a boyfriend called Steve Hardwick, so politely she declined his advances.

Bianchi then started work as a low paid guard for the Whatcom Security Agency and was given a very distinctive WSA truck complete with an orange flashing light bar on the roof to drive. It was here that Kenneth restyled himself as 'Captain Bianchi', even creating homemade business cards to allegedly prove he held such illustrious rank. He would also pose as a top Los Angeles modelling scout or photographer and try to entice and persuade young women into sex work. At this time, somewhat brazenly he was also making efforts to join the Sheriff's Reserves, and had started attending night classes. Since his late teens, Bianchi had wanted to be a cop but none of his applications had ever been successful. Again, we can see Bianchi reinventing himself.

On 8 January 1979, Bianchi approached Karen Mandic. Flashing his fake 'Captain Bianchi' business card he offered her an evening's well-paid work housesitting for a Dr. Catlow and his wife who lived at 334 Bayside Road, an upmarket location with uninterrupted panoramic views west across Bellingham Bay to the distant islands of Portage and Lummi. Bianchi explained that the job was worth a hundred dollars. It was an opportunity Karen could hardly refuse. She needed every dollar she could earn to support her education.

Upon learning what his girlfriend had agreed to do, Steve Hardwick was immediately suspicious. Karen, however, would have none of it, insisting that it was okay. She explained that the house was owned by a doctor and in a nice area. The doctor was going away with his family, but the alarm was not working. She had also asked a friend called Diane Wilder along for company. It was easy money she told Steve. All they had to do was wait until the burglar alarm repair people turned up later in the evening, then she would return to her shift at Fred Myer and cash up. Besides, Bianchi worked for WSA and it was a highly regarded firm. Even Hardwick, whose own father was a cop, knew that.

But Steve Hardwick, who could smell a latrine rat from miles away, was still highly suspicious, so he pressed Karen further. 'Don't worry,' she stressed, 'it's only for two hours. Everything will be OK. Ken has given my name to the insurance company who are paying the bill. I can't change anything now!'

When Karen failed to return to Fred Myer to cash up on the evening of Thursday, 11 January, the manager telephoned Hardwick who immediately drove to 334 Bayside Road. The property appeared deserted. Although Hardwick could not remember Bianchi's name, he did recall that he worked for WSA, so he phoned the night dispatcher Wendy Whitton, and requested any information on the Bayside account. She first checked to see if the tagged house keys for 334 Bayside Road were in the office but they were missing. She then informed the, now very concerned, Hardwick that she was not authorised to reveal details of her employer's business, promising him that she would call her boss, Randy Moa. But when she did alarm bells started to ring.

Moa and his partner Joe Parker had just completed a somewhat belated security check on Bianchi's resumé. In doing so they had spoken to Susan Bird, an attractive woman who lived locally. Susan had been shocked to hear that Bianchi had obtained work in the security business because he had recently suggested to her that because of her stunning figure she would make a good sex worker and that he could become her pimp. Susan was even more concerned when she found out that Ken had applied to join the Bellingham Police Department. Initially, Moa and Parker didn't believe Susan Bird, so she put them in touch with a girlfriend called Annie Kinneberg. Annie and her pal, Margie Lager, confirmed everything Susan had said relating to Bianchi, adding that he had also wanted to photograph lesbian models for clients he said he had back in LA. 'He's a kinky bastard,' Annie explained. 'He's living with a woman called Kellie, and they now have a little boy. That guy is weird, you know.'

Upon receiving the call from Wendy Whitton about the missing girl and the missing keys, Moa sprang into action. He radioed his night patrol officer, Steve Adams, and asked him to check out the Bayside Road address. Unfortunately, Steve went to number 302, the wrong house, where he knocked up the bleary-eyed owners who knew nothing at all. Then, having realised his mistake, he called the office and waited in his truck until the police turned up.

Meanwhile, Moa telephoned Bianchi at home. Ken denied all knowledge of the house-sitting job. He also denied knowing anyone called Karen Mandic or Diane Wilder, adding that he had been to a Sheriff's Reserve first-aid meeting that evening. Moa was not only confused but also becoming increasingly alarmed. He summoned Bianchi to the firm's office. Moa then contacted the instructor at the Sheriff's Reserve and learned that Ken had been lying. He had failed to turn up for the class. Moa was calling the Bellingham PD as Bianchi arrived at the office.

When detectives arrived at the WSA office, they asked Ken if he knew Karen Mandic or the twenty-seven-year-old Diane Wilder. Bianchi flatly denied knowing either before backtracking and saying, 'Maybe Karen.' A gut feeling told the officers that Bianchi was lying. He wouldn't look them straight in the eye. He appeared shifty and nervous. However, with little evidence to take him into custody, Bianchi was allowed to return home.

At 6 a.m. that morning, Bill Bryant, who was a university campus police officer, obtained a key to Karen's apartment. By the telephone, written in red ink, was a message in Diane's handwriting. It read: 'Karen. Ken B called. Phone 733-2884'. Picking up the scrap of paper, Bill decided to call the number. It turned out to be the WSA, and lo and behold, it was Bianchi who answered the phone. The rope was now tightening around this serial killer's neck.

'I know your voice,' said Bryant. 'You called Karen's apartment on Tuesday, and I told you that she wasn't in.' Once again, Ken denied knowing Karen Mandic, adding weakly that anyone could be using his name.

Bryant then phoned his own father, who was also a police officer, and Bryan Sr. subsequently called the Bellingham PD who re-interviewed Bianchi later that morning. Officers Geddes and Page confronted him with the note, and Bianchi reacted angrily, 'I'd sure like to know who has been using my name,' he snapped. 'I'm known. I was in the newspaper when I left Fred Myer to come here in charge of operations.' This was all utter bullshit. But even though Bianchi was now the chief suspect for the girls' abduction, the officers didn't have enough evidence yet to arrest him.

At 4.40 p.m. the same day, Karen's green Mercury Bobcat was found. Just a mile from the Bayside address, in a cul-de-sac in the then undeveloped Willow Drive, the vehicle contained the fully clothed bodies of Karen and Diane. At autopsy, it was determined that both had been raped and strangled with a ligature.

'The car was locked; however, the passenger door was only on the first catch and so I had no trouble getting into the vehicle that way. I opened both doors and took a closer look and the bodies of the two young ladies had been tossed in like sacks of potatoes, one thrown on top of the other.'

Crime scene officer Robert Knudsen to the
author during interview at the Bellingham PD

The shocking photos can be found on the internet if one so wishes to see them. With this grim discovery, an order went out for Bianchi's immediate arrest. Knowing that he might be armed and considered dangerous, police enlisted the help of Randy Moa. Moa radioed Ken in his truck, instructing his unwitting employee to check out a disused guard shack at the south terminal in a remote area of the docks. Moments after he arrived, Detective Terry Wight, brandishing a pistol, arrested him. Kenneth Alessio Bianchi would never be a free man again.

Eventually, Bianchi confessed to the killing of Diane Wilder and Karen Mandic (he has since flip-flopped arguing that he is totally innocent) but not before he claimed he suffered from multiple personality disorder and tried to lay the blame on one of those multiple personalities. He later retracted everything, to try and shift the blame onto Steve Hardwick and then Bill Bryant while at the same time appealing his conviction in the Washington courts.

The forensic evidence against Bianchi for the Bellingham homicides was overwhelming. As was the evidence against him and Angelo Buono for 'The Hillside Strangler' murders. There could be no ifs or buts about any of it. However, later during interviews and in correspondence with me Bianchi has continued to change his story. Bianchi wrote to me to tell me the reason he'd lied about his whereabouts the night Karen Mandic and Diane Wilder were killed:

'Chris, I hate confrontations. People only have their whereabouts checked when they are suspected of doing something wrong. So, knowing I hadn't done anything wrong, and had nothing to hide, I had given the original, short answer, about going to the Sheriff's Reserve class. That was simpler than the longer, true explanation. Besides, if I had killed the girls, I would have remembered it. I didn't, and that's what I kept telling the police.'

I asked Bianchi what his 'true explanation' was.

'That night it was snowing. I drove out to Mount Baker to check on a property but the blizzard and the terrible weather drove me back. But there was a man walking a dog so he must have seen my truck. If you can find him he will verify all that I say.'

I asked him what he did after he had turned back.

'Well I went back through Bellingham and headed seventy miles in the opposite direction to visit another place but I didn't make it coz of the weather, so I went home.'

He clearly forgot that when he did finally arrive home he took off his torn-at-the-crotch semen spattered jeans and threw them at Kellie ordering her to throw them away. Fortunately, she didn't for the jeans and his plaid shirt provided microscopic fibre evidence that not only had he been in the Catlows' house, but that he'd had intimate contact with Karen and Diane.

But Bianchi is capable of honesty sometimes and he has confessed his guilt but then he retracted it – he is a pathologically driven manipulating psychopath after all is said and done:

> 'They [Karen and Diane] were told to lie down and then they were separated, tied up and, individually, one by one, untied, undressed and I had sex with them. Then they were both dressed again. Then I killed them separately. I believe, Diane Wilder was first and Karen Mandic the second. Then they were carried out and put in the back of the car and driven to the cul-de-sac.'

Bianchi's inability to take responsibility for his crimes is example of deep-seated, psychopathic denial, and it is illustrative of his thought process around the time of the murders and the way his mind works today. He is a master manipulator and there is no better illustration of this than the lefty do-gooders who have actively supported Bianchi's parole applications over the years. The reader might like to now take a very, very stiff drink and sit down in a comfortable chair.

While in prison, residents of Walla Walla, Washington Gordon and Dorothy Otter, wrote to the Board of Prison Terms and Paroles, stating: 'From our observations of Mr Bianchi, we feel that he is sincere and a dedicated Christian man, who has a very positive attitude. He is always pleasant, takes an active part in the religious services, and he is concerned about the welfare of others.' Yep, you can bet on it that he is.

Pastor Dick Jewett, of the Stateline Seventh-Day Adventist Church in Milton-Freewater, Oregon wrote: 'I am filing this reference on behalf of Ken. He is a member in good standing of my church. I have baptised Ken myself and, after extensive interviews, I have satisfied my mind as to his sincerity. He is an active member and regular attendee at our services on the prison campus. His attitude and conduct at the present time is exemplary.'

A letter from churchgoer, Mrs Black, who seems equally as deranged as Pastor Jewett, says: 'We had the privilege of witnessing Ken Bianchi make a commitment to the Lord in Baptism. Ken appears to be very sincere, devoted and earnest. His views are conservative, but he never fails to look at both sides. He has always been polite and sensitive concerning this. He wants to attend college, which shows he has goals. My husband and I have been involved in the Prison Ministry for just over two years. We have written and talked to many prisoners. From these experiences we have learned to be fair judges of character. It is obvious to us that Kenneth Bianchi truly loves the Lord and his behaviour and attitude strongly proves it.' Thank the Lord that Mrs Black is not a trial judge, that's all I can say, bless her cotton socks.

At this late point, I might imagine you, dear reader, to be hyperventilating or rolling on your carpet with laughter, but it gets even better, trust me. Father Frederick Ellsworth, probably a well-meaning but utterly stark raving bonkers priest from the Christ the Healer Orthodox Mission, penned in support of Bianchi's parole: 'Ken is open, willing to share and quite responsive. I have two young daughters, and I would even welcome Ken into my home. He would fit in well with my family and his writing has been a hilit [sic].'

And the icing on the cake came from one Bruce Zicari from Penfield, New York, a tax consultant no less who felt that Ken needed his freedom, who wrote: 'I would certainly like to reiterate my confidence and high regard for Kenneth Bianchi, and I am certain that he has the capabilities to be successful at whatever field of endeavour he might choose.'

Of course, Ken's endeavours in the field of sado-sexual serial homicide had been highly successful, and he would have carried on being successful if all of these halfwits had got their way with the Board of Prison Terms and Paroles agreeing with them. Fortunately, the Board didn't agree with any of it. All of Bianchi's applications were torn up and thrown into a bin.

***

Peter William Sutcliffe

For the majority of the British population, Peter Sutcliffe's name is ingrained deep with our worst nightmares. The man known as the 'Yorkshire Ripper' *is* worthy of being included in this collection of monsters, for reasons soon to become apparent.

Of the thirty or so serial killers, mass murderers, spree killers and one-off destroyers of human life – be they men or women – whom I have interviewed and corresponded with over several decades, there is usually some tangible motivational peg I can hang my Sherlock Holmes deerstalker on. Please allow me to explain. In his 1931 book *Seven Murders*, Travers Christmas Humphreys QC – who later became an Old Bailey Judge – outlined the most common motives for murder.

1. The desire of avenging some real or fancied wrong.
2. Of getting rid of a rival or obnoxious connection.
3. Escaping from the pressure of pecuniary or other obligation.
4. Obtaining plunder or other coveted objects.

5. Preserving reputation.
6. Of gratifying some other selfish or malignant passion.

This set of motivations is still relevant today. What Humphreys is saying is that motive may be summed up more concisely as: money, hatred and sex. At the time the judge actually listed 'women', but we live in a more PC world these days so I changed this to 'sex'. So where does Peter Sutcliffe come into this? I suggest that his motives were broadly a combination of revenge and the gratification of his perverse passions. Here we find a man who was riddled through and through with the desire to avenge some real or fancied wrong, and, he was unquestionably a human monster with a pathological need to gratify *both* a selfish *and* a malignant passion.

It is interesting to consider the implications of point four. Many serial killers plunder, in that they take away 'trophies' from their crime scenes – it may be a lock of their victim's hair; items of underwear; jewellery or they may even record their kills with photographs to later further satisfy some malignant passion. Many killers, like Sutcliffe, take nothing physical away from their murders – but they will relive their crimes in their minds, often masturbating to these God-awful events. Is that not a form of trophy-taking too?

If we look deep into the psychopathology of many of these killers, we find something else – a man's motive may be good but his intention bad. Consider this: a loaf is stolen. The 'intention' was to steal and the act is therefore criminal, although the 'motive' – to save a starving child – was good. Generally speaking, however, the two are so entwined that it is difficult to separate them, and when such matters are brought up as a defence at trial they can provide for some mitigation for committing the wrongful act – thus a more lenient sentence being handed down.

Now I am going to confirm why Peter Sutcliffe deserves a special place in Hell. Born 2 June 1946, Sutcliffe also known as Peter Coonan was convicted of killing thirteen women and attempting to murder seven others between 1975 and 1980. This may seem an almost abhorrent thing to say but, as far as the other killers in this book are concerned, when we compare Sutcliffe with them he was a 'lightweight' – victim count wise.

'*Lightweight*? Christopher, how can you say such a thing?' I hear you scream. Let's back up a bit and consider that in many monsters, we find an underlying sexual motive. With Sutcliffe there is no apparent sexual motive at all.

This may seem rather odd, don't you think? Sutcliffe was a killer of young women, some were sex workers, others were not. But there is no evidence that he sexually molested them at all... he just killed them for killing's sake. Indeed, when we look deeper into his twisted psychopathology what we find is an utter hatred for women in general. Some will disagree with me, but I suggest that in killing in the way he did – bludgeoning with a hammer and stabbing with a screwdriver or other sharp instrument – he was gratifying some selfish or malignant passion. It was his perverted way of directing his anger at himself being such a loser onto others. In other words, he was punishing his victims for his own shortcomings. And Sutcliffe was born a loser from the outset.

John Sutcliffe was twenty-four and his wife Kathleen twenty-six, when their eldest child, weighing only five pounds was born. Peter would be joined by five siblings: Anne; Mick; Maureen; Jane and Carl. His parents were both Bingley locals and Kathleen, with her striking good looks, was considered quite a catch for the impulsive John.

Peter – even before he became an adult – often wondered jokingly if John Sutcliffe was his real father. Mr Sutcliffe was a self-proclaimed man's man, a famed local footballer, cricketer and actor – a man for all seasons. Peter, however, was shy, self-conscious and timid – characteristics that did not easily fit into the tough environment of the tough Ferncliffe Estate in the somewhat dour northern industrial town just six miles north of Bradford. It was Kathleen, the quiet and solid Catholic mother, who provided round-the-clock stability, seven days a week.

In 1957 he attended Cottingley Manor Roman Catholic School, which he hated because other children constantly bullied him. Soon after starting school, Peter played truant for two weeks. He would cling to his mother's skirts at home, following her everywhere in the house and round the streets. Although it has been said that he was quite intelligent, he failed his eleven-plus exams. His younger brothers – particularly Mick, three years Peter's junior – seemed to have inherited their father's appetite for life and the opposite sex. Their capacity to spend great chunks of the day consuming large quantities of beer and spirits played well with their peers in this tough place yet held no appeal to the weedy Peter who, although the eldest child, was the runt of the brood.

When he left school aged fifteen, traditionally the crossover point into manhood, Peter still confounded his family. He continued to be methodical, meticulous and fastidious, but he was now spending hours preening himself in the bathroom despite showing no interest in girls.

Self-preening is an interesting subject indeed. It can be a comforting action. It is a 'displacement activity' amongst primates, as psychiatrist and primatologist Alfonso Troisi noted. Well, we humans are all descended from apes – my late mother-in-law certainly was. In humans, Troisi noted that self-directed behaviour, like spending long periods in front of a mirror grooming – as well as actions such as aimless manipulation of objects (chewing pens, twisting rings) – is a sign of 'self-attraction' and can be used as an indicator of 'stressful stimuli'. It's a form of self-loving, of soothing of one's subconsciously fragile ego, to make oneself more presentable to others. We find habitual self-preening is common amongst narcissists. In extreme narcissists who exhibit antisocial personality traits it can develop into a fully blown sociopathy/psychopathy.

Peter's self-preening became a Sutcliffe family joke and word soon spread around the community that he was gay. One of his earliest jobs was as a gravedigger at a cemetery in Bingley. During this time he developed a macabre sense of humour, mainly as a way of playing down this somewhat gruesome job. He would even quip: 'thousands of people are below me where I work now.' His shrill and wildly uncontrollable, almost childish laughter, would surprise those who heard it for the first time from such an apparently serious young man. On one occasion he pretended to be a corpse, lying down on a slab with a shroud over himself, making moaning noises when his workmates appeared. They regarded him as inscrutable. His trim, dark beard earned him the name 'Jesus'. He used to boast that he had removed gold and jewellery from corpses he then buried. Later, at his trial, he claimed that he had heard the voice of God while he was digging a grave. This voice, he alleged, came from the top of a hill. He had followed the echoing and mumbling words to the cross-shaped headstone of a man called Bronislaw Za Polski – who, incidentally, had met the real God on 19 June 1965 – and the voice told Sutcliffe to go out on the streets and kill women. Sutcliffe got himself fired from his menial job of digging holes. Only God knows how difficult it must be to get sacked from simply digging holes, but Peter managed it. The fact was that Peter, aka 'Jesus', was bone-idle and was always late for work.

Like so many men who feel they need to compensate for their physical shortcomings, he took up bodybuilding. He went on a course of 'bulk-builder' foods and would spend an hour most evenings training with his 'Bullworker'. At his local pub, The Royal Standard, Sutcliffe would sit bolt upright, knees neatly together. Those who engaged him in conversation found him creepily still – only his eyes would move. It was apparent to Peter, and everyone else, that he *was* different.

Sutcliffe met sixteen-year-old, Sonia Szurma in his local pub. She was the daughter of Czechoslovakian parents. Sutcliffe's eight-year courtship of Sonia was tortuous to say the least. On Sundays, they sat in chairs in the family's dining room lost in their own chitchat, only speaking to the others when it was totally unavoidable. His brother Mick and Sonia made no secret of their personal dislike for each other. Mick thought she was too bossy and was always talking Peter down. She would snap at him: 'Peter, will you shut up.' She was domineering, overpowering, and this fact weighed heavily on this man's already fragile ego. He had always been the weakest of his own brood, now he would become the downtrodden in their marriage. So he started to harbour a deep-seated desire for revenge. He could not exact his vengeance on those closest to him, so he would seek it elsewhere.

Sutcliffe was a mummy's boy and had always stuck up for his mother, sympathising with the hard time he believed his domineering father gave her. However, before he left the family home, his faith in her traditional Catholic purity was smashed apart. His father had discovered that Kathleen was having an affair with a neighbour, a local policeman. This made the patriarch – 'The Man about Bingley' – look like a fool and a man who couldn't even satisfy his meek, downtrodden wife. John Sutcliffe had arranged for the children, including Peter and his then bride-to-be Sonia, to be present at a Bingley hotel for a grand confrontation. Kathleen had been fooled into believing that she was to meet her boyfriend in the bar, only to be forced by her husband to show everyone the new nightdress she had bought to please her lover that night. Peter was devastated. More so because he had also discovered earlier that Sonia, too, had a secret boyfriend. He hinted to his father that he understood how wild and humiliated he must feel. At long last, Peter and his father had something in common. They now believed that no woman could be trusted.

Since his son's trial and conviction, John Sutcliffe has said that he believed the trauma of his mother's affair created the 'Yorkshire Ripper' inside Peter: 'It shook him rigid. He worshipped his mother and I think now that what I did turned his mind.' One psychiatrist involved in the case who evaluated Peter Sutcliffe agreed, explaining that Kathleen's affair could have moved him into a 'acute psychotic state'.

There could be much mileage in the idea that maybe this sad event did trigger something in Sutcliffe, but my own considerable experience, having worked with serial killers over at least three decades, tells me quite the opposite. I say this because millions of youngsters suffer similar traumas and do not become such beasts. Furthermore, I see some belated, and quite unnecessary self-blame here from John Sutcliffe who had always treated his son like the pipsqueak of the family. We only have to witness Peter Sutcliffe's later behaviour to show that here we find one of the most manipulative serial killers in British criminal history. It is of some significance that later that same year, Sutcliffe carried out his first known attack in Bradford. He hit a sex worker over the head with a stone in a sock following an argument over a £10 note. This was a terrible portent for things to come. And it is instructive to note that here he is using a stone in a sock – an unusual choice of weapon and one that he must have prepared beforehand. It tells us that he had no intention of having sex with the woman, he was seeking to punish a female, to vent his pent-up fury upon her. Sutcliffe's second confirmed attack took place in Keighley on Saturday, 5 July 1975 when he used a ball-peen hammer to knock a thirty-four-year-old woman called Anna Rogulskyj, who was walking alone at night, unconscious. He then slashed her stomach with a knife.

Olive Smelt, aged forty-six, was an office cleaner. She was attacked on 15 August 1975. She was enjoying her regular Friday night out on the town with her friends and having a few drinks at the Royal Oak public house in Halifax's town centre. Before heading home, she called at a fish and chip shop to get a late supper for her husband, Harry, and her family. Peter Sutcliffe and his friend Trevor Birdsall were also out drinking that night and they ended up also at the Royal Oak. Sutcliffe started loud-mouthing at the bar, saying that it was a 'prostitutes' bar'. He singled out Olive Smelt, and said to Birdsall, 'I bet she's on the game!' Then, while on his way to use the toilet, he said something very similar straight to her face. Instantly she put him in his place. Just before closing time, Olive and one of her friends met two men she knew and they offered to give her a lift home. They drove her as far as a layby in Boothtown Road, just a short walk to her home.

Sutcliffe and Birdsall had now also left the Royal Oak and had started driving towards Bradford. They were less than a mile from the pub when Sutcliffe spotted a woman walking down Woodside Road, and as she turned into a narrow lane, he recognised her, saying to Birdsall: 'That is the prostitute we saw in the public house.'

Birdsall noticed that Sutcliffe put his hand down the side of his driver's seat. Peter said that he was going to speak with someone, then he went round to the back of the car. It appeared to Birdsall that he wasn't heading in the same direction as the lone woman. In reality, however, Sutcliffe ran down a parallel alley to the one Olive was walking along. The time was now 11.45 p.m.

When Sutcliffe caught up with Olive he said: 'Weather's letting us down, isn't it?' to which she replied: 'Yes.' Moments later he struck her twice on the head with a hammer – her skull was crushed like an eggshell – and made two slash marks about six to eight inches long at the top of her buttocks with a knife or a hacksaw blade he was carrying. Disturbed by a car coming down the road with its headlights on, he fled the scene and returned to his car and Birdsall about twenty minutes later. He would later tell the police that his intention had been to kill Olive.

Olive was found in the alleyway and rushed first to Halifax Infirmary, later to Leeds Infirmary, where, after brain surgery, she spent the next ten days. She described her attacker as about aged thirty, five foot and ten inches in height, slightly built, with dark hair and some beard or stubble on his face. The following day, Birdsall read in the *Bradford Telegraph & Argus* about the apparently motiveless attack on Olive Smelt. She hadn't been sexually assaulted or had anything stolen, but he had smelt a rat thinking that Sutcliffe had to have been responsible, but did absolutely zilch about his strong suspicions.

Although she more-or-less made a full recovery from her terrible injuries, Olive's physical mobility was never the same again. In April 2011, Olive, aged eighty-two, died in the Huddersfield Royal Infirmary after a short illness.

If we were able to put ourselves into the psychopathological mindset of Peter Sutcliffe at this time, we would see a developing contempt for women. The two initial attacks on women were, we might say, 'practice runs'. He was learning what would become his murderous MO. But with Olive he now had acknowledged intent to kill and this time he not only used his hammer but also a sharp instrument, in an attempt to finish her off. The fact that Olive had survived had cheated him of his wicked goal he reasoned. This frustrated him and angered him more. Next time around he vowed he would do the job properly, and he would exact his revenge on the next woman who fell prey.

Wilma McCann, aged twenty-eight, was a strawberry-blonde mother who was murdered in Leeds, on Thursday, 30 October. She was a Scottish lass who lived with her four children in a Chapeltown council house. She was struck down just a hundred yards from home in Scott Hall Avenue. Wilma's bone-chilling murder was committed on a bone-chillingly cold Yorkshire night. Her body was found by milkman, Alan Routledge, and his younger brother Paul who were shivering on their clattering rounds in the icy fog of the October dawn. As he peered through the freezing mist to see his way past the bleak recreation ground just off the Harrogate Road, he saw a shapeless bundle huddled on the frosty wintry grass. At first, he thought it was probably only a Guy Fawkes as Bonfire Night was just a week away – but something made Alan cautiously go over to investigate.

The woman's corpse was sprawled, face upwards, her hair matted with blood. Her jacket and blouse were open, her bra pulled up, her trousers were pulled down below the knees, although her pants were still in position. Her chest and stomach were lacerated with fourteen stab wounds. Later, the pathologist report revealed that she had been attacked from behind and dealt two heavy hammer-like blows. One of the impacts had shattered the back of her skull. The stabs were inflicted after death.

'I thought "God, what have I done?" I realised I would be in serious trouble. I thought the best way out of the mess was to make sure she could not tell anybody.'

Peter Sutcliffe on the murder of Wilma McCann

Wilma often hitchhiked home after nights on the town and she had been drinking throughout the evening before she was murdered. At postmortem, Professor David Gee determined that during her last hours she had consumed twelve to fourteen measures of spirits. On that fatal night, Wilma wore her favourite outfit – a pink blouse, white flares and a dark blue bolero jacket. She left her home at 7.30 p.m., instructing her eldest daughter, Sonje, aged nine, to keep the three younger children in bed and the front door locked. Upon leaving, Wilma walked past the nearby Prince Phillip Playing Fields, and headed for the pubs and clubs. Drinking whiskies and beer, she was seen in the Regent, the Scotsman, the White Swan and the Royal Oak. Closing time was at 10.30 p.m., and now wobbly on her feet she headed to the 'Room at the Top' nightclub, where she stayed until shortly before 1 a.m. She headed home carrying a container of curry and chips.

Even though it was a short walk back to her place Wilma staggered around recklessly signalling to traffic in hopes of getting a ride home. She flagged down a lorry headed for the M62, but the driver slammed his door shut and drove off.

Below is an extract from Sutcliffe's confession to police, dated 4–5 January 1981. Source material (details): Burn, Cross, Jones. Source material (quotes): *Statement of Peter William Sutcliffe*, Bilton.

'That was the incident that started it [the murders] all off. I was driving through Leeds late at night, I'd been to somewhere having a couple of pints, you'll know the date better than me. It was Wilma McCann. I was in a Ford Capri, 'K' registered, a lime green one with a black roof with a sun grill in the back window. I saw this woman thumbing a lift where the Wetherby Road branches to the right, but you can carry straight on. She was wearing some white trousers and a jacket. I stopped and asked her how far she was going. She said: 'Not far, thanks for stopping.' And she jumped in. I was in quite a good mood and we were talking on the way. She said something about, just before we stopped, about did I want business. To me I didn't know what she meant by that. I asked her to explain and straightaway a scornful tone came into her voice, which took me by surprise because she had been so pleasant. She said: 'Bloody Hell, do I have to spell it out?' She said it as though it was a challenge. My reaction was to agree to go with her.

'She told me where to park the car. It was just off this road, we turned left, we came to this field [Prince Phillip Playing Fields]. We sat there for a minute talking then all of a sudden her tone changed and she said: 'Well, what are we waiting for, let's get on with it,' before we stopped she said that it would cost a fiver. I was a bit surprised. I was expecting it to be a bit romantic. I think she had been drinking because she was being irrational. I couldn't have intercourse in a split second, I had to be aroused.

'At this point she opened the car door and got out. She slammed the door and shouted: "I'm going, it's going to take you all fucking day!" She shouted something like, "You're fucking useless."

'I suddenly felt myself seething with rage. I got out of the car wanting to hit her to pay her back for the insult. I went to her and said: "Hang on a minute, don't go off like that." She was only three or four strides away, she turned and came back to me. She said something like: "Oh, you can fucking manage it now, can you?" She sounded like she was taunting me.

'I said: "There's not much room in the car, can we do it on the grass?" This was with my idea of hitting her. She said: "I'm not going to do it here bloody well next to the car." With that, she stormed up the hill into the field.

'I had a toolbox on the seat of the car and I took a hammer out of the toolbox. I followed her into the field. I took my coat off and carried it over my arm. I had the hammer in my right hand. I put my coat on the grass. She sat down on the coat. She unfastened her trousers. She said: "Come on then, get it over with." I said: "Don't worry, I will."

'I then hit her with the hammer on the head. I was stood up at that time. I think I hit her on the top of her head. I hit her once or twice on the head. She fell down flat on her back and started making a horrible noise like a moaning gurgling noise.

'I thought, "God what have I done?" I knew I had gone too far. I ran to the car intending to drive off. I sat in the car for a while. I could see her arm moving. I was in a numb panic. I still had my hammer in my hand. I put it back in my toolbox.

'I half expected her to get up, and realised I would be in serious trouble. I thought the best way out of the mess was to make sure she couldn't tell anybody. I took a knife out of the toolbox. It had a wood handle with one sharp side. The blade was about seven inches long and three-quarters-of-an-inch wide.

'I went back to her. She was still lying on her back. I thought that to make certain she was dead I would stab her in places like the lungs and the throat. I stabbed her at least four times, once in the throat. Before I stabbed her in the body, I pulled her blouse or whatever it was and her bra, so I could see where I was stabbing her, just to make sure she wouldn't tell anyone.

'What a stupid thing to do just to keep somebody quiet. If I was thinking logical at the time, I would have stopped and told someone I'd hit her with a hammer. That was the turning point. I realised I overreacted at the time. Nothing I have done since then affected me like this.

'After I stabbed her I went back to the car. I remember that I'd taken my coat off the ground when I hit her with the hammer, and I'd taken the coat back to the car. I started the car and shot off backwards along the narrow road leading to the road [Scott Hall Road – A61], swing the car around, and drove away towards Leeds. I drove home as soon as possible.

'I was then living with my mother-in-law at 44 Tanton Crescent, Clayton, Bradford. I was very frightened and don't even remember driving there. I thought I was bound to get caught. I parked my car outside the house. I'm trying to remember if it was my mother-in-law's house I was living at then. I've thought it out now, it must have been her house. I looked over my clothing before I went into the house. I went straight to the bathroom and washed my hands and went to bed … the next day I saw it on the TV news about the murder and

I felt sick and I still half expected a knock on the door by the police. I carried on trying to act as normal, living with my wife and in-laws. At that time I worked at Common Road Tyre Services at Okenshaw. After that first time, I developed and built up a hatred for prostitutes in order to justify within myself the reason why I had attacked and killed Wilma McCann.'

Sonje had followed her mum's orders faithfully until five o'clock the next morning when the tearful clamouring from her siblings, and her own anxiety, goaded her into action. Bleary-eyed and anxious, she took her younger brother, Richard, aged seven, and went for help. They were discovered, shivering at the local bus stop, hugging each other for warmth and reassurance.

Despite the condition of Wilma's body, the police thought there was no sexual motive for her murder, which, on its face seems correct. Her purse, the clasp bearing the word 'Mummy', inscribed by Sonje, was missing. In the absence of any motive, the police then witlessly treated Wilma's killing as a callous by-product of robbery. Investigations were set up but bore no fruit. But what we can take away from Sutcliffe's statement *is* the fact that he had attacked prostitutes before this homicide – almost killing Olive Smelt – that he was trawling the red light district of Leeds for a victim. His intention not to secure a sexual encounter at all – he simply wanted to kill a woman for the sake of it and the sheer bloodthirsty fun of it.

Emily Jackson was a forty-two-year-old wife and mother. She was murdered in Leeds on Tuesday,

20 January 1976. At this point, it is worth looking a little closer into Emily's recent narrative for here we find a woman who worked alongside her husband, Sydney, a roofing contractor, doing his paperwork and driving the old Commer van for him on jobs since he didn't hold a driver's licence. Around the previous Christmas, Sydney's work dried up and due to the financial pressures Emily turned to sex work – making money from the men she might pick up in their regular excursions to local pubs. And it was her habit to cruise the dismal streets of Chapeltown looking for clients, or she would sometimes leave the van in a car park and go off with clients in their vehicles. Outwardly maintaining a respectable existence, she lived with her husband and three children in Back Green Street, Churwell, west of Leeds, and five miles to the west of the red light district, Chapeltown.

On 20 January, Emily and Sydney arrived at the Gaiety public house along the Roundhay Road at around 6.15 p.m. – an acknowledged watering hole for local irregulars and their would-be 'clientele'. However, within minutes of their arrival Emily left her husband in the main lounge and went fishing for business. Less than an hour later, she was seen climbing into a Land Rover in the car park – that was the last time she was seen alive. At closing time, Sydney Jackson, still alone, drank up and took a taxi home, perhaps assuming that his wife had found a 'boyfriend' for the night.

It was still dark the next morning when a worker on an early shift noticed a 'huddled bulky shape' on the ground covered with a coat not far from the city centre. The body was lying between two derelict houses in Manor Street in Chapeltown, close to an industrial estate. Detective Chief Superintendent Dennis Hoban, head of Leeds CID, told reporters that the woman had suffered severe head injuries and other injuries, on which he did not wish to elaborate. He did, however, say that the killer was 'sadistic and possibly a sexual pervert.' No prizes to be awarded for Lt. Columbo-style detective skills here, then.

Emily's body, like Wilma McCann's, was sprawled on her back. Her breasts were exposed, her legs apart and her pants left on. She, too, had been dealt two massive blows to the head with a heavy hammer. Sutcliffe had stabbed Emily over *fifty* times, gouging her back with a Phillips screwdriver. Marks on the ground showed how he had dragged the body to the spot where she was found. Her handbag was lying close by – nothing appeared to have been taken.

One senior detective admitted that the sight of such a ferocious attack had left him numb with horror, adding 'whoever this bastard is, he deserves a special place in Hell.' Perhaps more sickening was the impression of a heavy ribbed Wellington boot stamped on Emily's right thigh which was later identified as being from a Dunlop Warwick (size 7, no larger than 8). Curiously, the autopsy revealed a strong indication that sexual activity had taken place, but *before* the attack and, *not with her killer.* The most likely conclusion being that Emily had sex with the driver of the Land Rover, then – with money in her purse – she was on her way home when Sutcliffe came upon her. When Sutcliffe was interviewed by police on 4/5 January 1981, he had this to say:

'This time I drove to Leeds looking for a prostitute because I felt I could not justify what I had done previously and I felt an inner compulsion to kill a prostitute. This was about a month before Christmas.

'I drove to Leeds in my Capri about 8 or 9 p.m. I saw a woman dressed in an overcoat trying to stop drivers from the pavement on the road that leads to Wetherby Road. It was near some phone boxes. I stopped and wound the window down. I said, "How much?" She said, "Five pounds." I remember when she got in the car there was an overpowering smell of cheap perfume and sweat, this served me all the more to hate this woman even though I didn't even know her. Looking back, I can see how the first murder had unhinged me completely.

'She was heavily built and had brown hair. She said she knew where we could go. I knew from the outset I didn't want intercourse with her. I just wanted to get rid of her. At that time, I was dressed in my working clothes, at that time I used to wear Wellington boots at work.

'At her direction, I turned the car round and drove back the way we'd come. We had gone just about 400 yards and she told me to turn left again and drove behind some old buildings – it was a cul-de-sac. I couldn't bear even going through the motions of having sex with this woman. On the journey she told me that she could drive.

'I wanted to do what I'd had in mind as soon as possible. I remember turning on the ignition again so the red warning light came on, and I pretended that the car would not start. I said I would have to lift up the bonnet to sort it out. I asked her if she would give me a hand. We both got out of the car. I lifted up the bonnet of the car. I had picked up a hammer which I had put near my seat for the purpose. I told her I could not see properly without a torch. She offered to use her cigarette lighter to shine under the bonnet.

'She was holding her lighter. I took a couple of steps back and I hit her over the head with the hammer. I think I hit her twice. She fell down onto the road. I took hold of her hands or wrists and pulled her into a yard which had rubbish in it. I then made sure she was dead by taking a screwdriver and stabbing her repeatedly. I pulled her dress up and her bra before I stabbed her to make it easier. To be truthful, I pulled her clothes up in order *to satisfy some sort of sexual revenge* [author's italics] as on reflection on her [sic] as I had done on McCann.

'I stabbed her frenziedly, without thought, with a Phillips screwdriver all over her body… I was seething with hate for her. I remember picking up a piece of wood from the yard, about two or three feet long … and pushing it up against her vagina with it [sic] as she lay on the back. I cannot recall taking her knickers down... I threw the wood away in the yard.'

This author has highlighted '*to satisfy some sort of sexual revenge*', as this, I believe, was his homicidal *raison d'être* from the outset. By now, he had formed the opinion that the mother he had loved so dearly had, to his mind, turned out to be a whore for having an affair behind his father's back. This had angered him bitterly, because she had betrayed him too.

This resentment also applied to his wife, Sonia, for she had also allegedly cheated on him while they were engaged. This suspicion did nothing for his over-inflated ego. But he was trapped in a relationship with Sonia, a strong-willed young woman who treated him with much disdain. Sonia still ruled the roost. She would snap her fingers when she wanted something, and would talk him down in the company of others. Like so many serial killers, when they cannot hurt those closest to them they take out their revenge on others, or people that these monsters *perceive* to be in the same image.

Marcella Claxton, aged twenty, was attacked by Sutcliffe in Leeds, on Sunday, 9 May 1976. She lived on one of the terraces of back-to-back houses off Roundhay Road which borders on Chapeltown, and the even more rundown district, Harehills. Marcella was a sex worker.

The facts about this attack are varied, often confusing. What we do know is that on Saturday, 8 May, Marcella says that she had been at a late night drinking party in Chapeltown and had left around 4 a.m. She was drunk, and this is Sutcliffe's account which differs considerably from what Marcella later told police:

> 'I picked her up in the Chapeltown area. She asked me if I was the police. I said, "No, do I really look like a policeman?" She decided to get into the car, and suggested where we could go. We ended up in what I now know as Soldiers Field. [Author's note: Marcella strongly denied soliciting for business that night, however Sutcliffe's statement does have a solid ring of truth about it.]
>
> 'We got out of the car at my suggestion. She went behind some trees to urinate and she took off her trousers whilst leaning against a tree, and she sat down on the grass and suggested we start the ball rolling. Straight after she said this I hit her with the hammer. Again, I don't know what it was this time, but I just couldn't bring myself to hit her again for some reason or another and I just let her walk away, possibly to tell the nearest policeman or passerby what had happened.'

Covered in blood from her wounds, Marcella managed to stagger to a nearby phone box to call for help. She told police that, while waiting in the phone box she saw her attacker return and start looking around. She thought that he was coming back to finish her off. She required extensive brain surgery and needed fifty-two stitches to close the wounds in her head, and she also lost the child she was carrying, later testifying to this at Sutcliffe's trial.

Source material (details): Burn, Cross, Fido, Jones, Kinsley & Smyth. Source material (quotes): Bilton, Yallop.

Irene Richardson, aged twenty-eight, was murdered in Leeds on 5 February 1977, at almost exactly the same spot as the previous attack on Marcella Claxton.

Irene was homeless and well and truly down on her luck. She earned money as a sex worker but had spent most of the previous days almost penniless. She had taken to hanging around street corners looking for a customer. She was last seen alive at 11.15 p.m. leaving a seedy rooming house on Cowper Street where she had taken a room, saying that she was going to Tiffany's public house and 'Bali Hai' disco in Leeds town centre.

Meanwhile, Sutcliffe had spent part of his evening looking, without success, for a victim. Not far from the Gaiety pub he spotted Irene. He pulled up and she jumped in without saying a word. When Sutcliffe told her that he might not want her, she replied that she would show him a good time for a fiver. They drove a mile along Roundhay Road into Roundhay Park then continued on until they reached Soldiers Field where he had previously attacked Marcella Claxton.

Peter Sutcliffe describes what took place in his confession dated 4/5 January 1981. It makes for grim reading.

'The next one I did was Irene Richardson.
I then owned a red Corsair and also a white

Corsair ... I had both of these at the same time and I honestly cannot remember which one I was using that night.

'I drove to Leeds after the pubs shut. It was my intention to find a prostitute to make it one less. [Note: how this beast describes his victims with complete callousness.] I saw this girl walking in some cross streets in the middle of the vice estate near a big club. I stopped my car and she got in without me saying a word. ... She told me to drive to the park. We came to this big field on my left. I drove off the road onto the field near some toilets. She wanted to use the toilets, so she got out and went over to them. She came back and said they were locked. Before she went to the toilet she took off her coat and placed it on the ground. When she came back she said she would have a wee on the ground. She took her boots off... then she crouched down to have a pee. By this time, I was out of my car and I had my hammer in my hand.

'As she was crouching down, I hit her on the head from behind, at least twice, maybe three times. She fell down. I then lifted up her clothes and slashed her in the lower abdomen and also slashed her throat [with a Stanley knife]. I left her laying face down and I covered her up with her coat. I put her knee boots on top of her before I covered her up. I heard a voice nearby and saw a car being driven away from a block of flats, so I drove away.

'By this time, after the Richardson killing, prostitutes became an obsession with me and I couldn't stop myself... it was like some sort of drug.'

John Bolton was out jogging across Soldiers Field, when, at 7.30 a.m., he spotted the body of Irene Richardson on the ground at the rear of a sports pavilion, near some trees. At first, he thought it was someone who had been taken ill, so he asked her: 'What's the matter?' Then, after he brushed her hair aside, he saw 'blood on her neck and her eyes were glazed and staring.' He ran to one of the nearby houses and called the police who arrived to find her lying face down, her hands under her stomach, and her head turned to the left. Her long hair was matted with blood which hid the stab wounds in her neck and throat. The imitation-suede, fur-trimmed coat she'd been wearing had been draped over her buttocks and legs, with only her feet showing. Her calf-length brown boots had been carefully placed over her thighs. Her bra was still in position, but her skirt had been pulled up and her tights pulled down. Besides the neck and throat wounds, there had been three stabs to the stomach, one six and three-quarter inches long. All were severe downward strokes that had caused her intestines to spill out of the wounds. Irene had been effectively disembowled. At autopsy, the pathologist determined that Irene had had sex within the twenty-four hours before her death and she was wearing two pairs of knickers because she was menstruating.

It goes without saying that all monsters like Peter Sutcliffe deserve a special place in Hell. And there is a reason that he gained the moniker 'Ripper' because Sutcliffe's *modus operandi* reminds us in so many ways of our Victorian 'Jack the Ripper'. Like Sutcliffe, Jack was not a sex killer in the true sense either – at the heart of his motive was a deep-seated hatred and a need for revenge. However, it is true to say that many serial murderers can only achieve orgasm during this ferocious killing phase, yet there is no evidence to suggest that this was the case with 'The Yorkshire Ripper'. Indeed, the stabs to the stomachs of his victims tell us a bit more about Sutcliffe's psychopathology for he is destroying that part of a female that bears children – the lower abdomen. This is all so similar to the murders committed by 'Jack the Ripper' back in Victorian times. The attacks amounted to a violation and total destruction of the womb – no more no less. Peter and Sonia were involuntarily childless as he had a very low sperm count. To be blunt, here we have a man with a massively self-inflated ego, the preener, the bullshitter, and self-professed ladies' man – but he could never quite live up to his own vision of himself.

We could, if we so wished, easily dismiss the hammer blows to the head as merely being expedient knockdown blows designed to bring his victim down and quickly. But the blows inflicted by Sutcliffe were so heavy that they crushed skulls like eggshells. I have seen the same ferocity used by other serial killers I have interviewed: notably Harvey Louis 'The Hammer' Carignan. During my exclusive interview with him at the Minnesota Correctional Facility (MCF) Stillwater, Harvey told me that he wanted to destroy his victims' heads because their minds 'played games' with him. In part, I see this vengeance enacted again and again in Sutcliffe's MO.

It has also been argued by many observers that Sutcliffe's motive was one of needing sexual relief culminating in ejaculation. I suggest that this is incorrect, although one of his victims told police that he ejaculated on the grass after he had almost killed her. I find this somewhat difficult to comprehend, for here is a woman in such a terrible state, physically and mentally, that recalling something like that would, perhaps, have been the last thing on her mind.

So, can the reader see a little deeper inside Sutcliffe's head now? Can you now start to see what is making him tick? Oh, what an amoral, disgusting little prick!

Patricia Atkinson, known as Tina, was thirty-two. She was murdered in Bradford, Saturday, 23 April 1977, becoming the second woman to die that year at Sutcliffe's hands. Tina lived at Flat 3, 9 Oak Avenue and, on that fateful night, she dressed in her favourite outfit: blue denim jeans, short leather jacket, and a largely unbuttoned blue shirt and visited 'The Perseverance' public house, in Lumb Lane. Here she drank heavily. Tina was a sex worker and, after a while, she left that pub and ambled along to another of her favourite pick-up bars, 'The Carlisle' at 86 Carlisle Road. Here, however, the manager thought better of serving her more alcohol and she left at 10.20 p.m. The staff watched her stagger towards the exit, and set off towards another pub, The International, which closed at around 11 p.m. Other sex workers saw her walking unsteadily. This was when Tina was spotted by 'The Yorkshire Ripper' wearing jeans, a pair of Doc Martin boots and primed to kill.

In his confession of 4/5 January 1981, and in response to specific police questions, Sutcliffe had this to say:

'I drove off Lumb Lane into Church Street [Gracechurch Street]. I knew this was a prostitute area. I was in my Corsair, either the white one or the red one.

'I saw this woman [Atkinson] in St Pauls Road, at a junction with another road. She appeared drunk and was banging on the roof of a white Mini and was shouting and bawling, "Fuck off!" and such things to the driver, who then drove off at speed. I pulled up to her and stopped and without asking me she jumped in the car. She said, "I fucking told him where to get off!" She told me where to go. We turned right at the junction with Manningham Lane, turned left down Queen's Road, left into Oak Avenue, and turned second left and stopped at her flat.

'She told me she lived alone. I parked up outside her flat and she got out and went in. I picked up a hammer as I got out of the car. I remember this was a claw hammer that I had bought at the Clayton hardware shop.

'I followed her into the flat. She closed the curtains, and I hung my coat on the hook on the back of the door. She took off her coat and sat on the bed, her back was slightly towards me. I went up to her and hit her on the back of the head. She fell off the bed onto the floor. I picked her up and put her back on the bed. That was the first time I had noticed the red blood, before it had always been dark, but this time in the light I saw lots of blood on the bed and on the floor. When she was on the floor I hit her twice, or three times, before I put her on the bed. I pulled the bedclothes back before I put her on the bed.

'She had already pulled her jeans down before I hit her. I pulled her clothes up and I hit her several times on her stomach and back with the claw part of the hammer and I saw that I was making marks on her body doing this. I then covered her up the bedclothes [sic]. I think she was laying face down or on her side when I left her.

'When I first hit her, she was making a horrible gurgling sound, and she carried on making this noise even though I'd hit a few more times. She was still making this gurgling sound when I left, but I knew she would not be in a state to tell anyone.'

'I talked to her saying I was sorry for what I had done.
It was the first time I had apologised to someone I had killed.'
Peter Sutcliffe: on the killing of Jayne MacDonald

Jayne MacDonald was sixteen years old. She was murdered in Leeds, on Sunday, 26 June 1977. Around 2 a.m., Sutcliffe spotted the lone girl wearing a gingham skirt emerging into the street lights of Chapeltown. He watched Jayne as she passed the imposing Hayfield public house, turning left down Reginald Terrace – one of the many side streets running off the main road. Parking his white Ford Corsair, he got out and began to follow her. The body of Jayne was found lying by a wall at 9.45 a.m., by a group of children making their way to the adventure playground in Reginald Terrace. Jayne had been struck on the back of the head, dragged twenty yards from the pavement and then hit twice more. She was then stabbed once in the back and repeatedly through the chest.

Jayne had only just left school and worked in the shoe department of a local supermarket. On the night she was killed, she had been with friends in Leeds and the attack took place on her way back to her parents' home, just a few hundred yards from where her body was found. She was the first victim who the investigators did not link to sex work to be killed by the Ripper.

Maureen Long was forty-two. She was attacked in Bradford, on Sunday, 10 July 1977, only two weeks after Sutcliffe killed Jayne MacDonald. She had left her Farsley, Leeds, home the previous evening for a night on the town in Bradford, and she visited a number of public houses. At one of them she ran into her estranged husband and they agreed that she go to his place in Laisterdyke, Bradford, later that night. First, she would go to the Mecca ballroom, now renamed Tiffany's, in Manningham. Here, Maureen was seen in the 'Bali Hai' disco, where people recalled her dancing with a number of men. She appeared very drunk by the time she left just after 2 a.m. Her body was discovered at 8.30 a.m., when two women walking near waste ground heard her feeble cries, which at first they mistook for a whimpering dog. Her girdle, pants and tights had been pulled down. She had suffered one blow to the back of her head and stab wounds to her chest, stomach and back, including one slash that went from her breasts to below her navel.

In his confession to police dated 4/5 January 1981, Sutcliffe had this to say:

> 'I was driving along Manningham Lane towards the city centre on a Saturday night in July 1977. It was late at night. I saw her [Long] walking on the same side as the Mecca towards Bradford Centre. She was wearing a maxi length dress and a jacket sort of coat.
>
> 'She was just past the hamburger stand when I saw her. I stopped my car and said, "Are you going far?" She said, "Are you giving me a lift?" I said, "If you want one." She told me where she lived, and that she lived with a man who was an ex-boxer and that he was a spoilsport and would not take her to the Mecca. ... She told me that if there was no one in the house we could go in.'

Apparently because someone else was in the house, Maureen returned to Sutcliffe's car and according to him she directed him into Bowling Back Lane, before they turned right down a cobbled street where they stopped. Sutcliffe went on to say:

> 'There was some spare unlevelled land on the right. She got out of the car and she was going for a piss first and she went down to the spare land and crouched down and had a piss.'

It was at this moment that he hit Maureen Long with his hammer. She slumped to the ground and he dragged her by the hands further onto the wasteland where he stabbed her three or four times in the chest with a knife. Thinking he had done enough he left her then drove away. Maureen survived and when Sutcliffe heard of this the following day he would later tell police that he thought that it would be the end of him. His concerns proved to be unfounded as Maureen suffered from amnesia and was unable to provide a description of her assailant. Nevertheless, so worried was Sutcliffe that she might remember his white Corsair, he eventually stripped it of parts which he used to replace parts in his red car all of which conflicts with his notion that his killings were frenzied and somehow beyond his control.

Jean Bernadette Jordon was also known as Jean Royle, and was twenty-one years old when she was murdered in Manchester. The date was Saturday, 1 October 1977 and Jean, known as a sex worker, was last seen alive climbing into Sutcliffe's red Corsair near her home in Moss Side. She accepted £5 in advance and directed him to some land two miles away between allotments and the Southern Cemetery much favoured by sex workers as a discreet place to do business. A few yards from the car, Sutcliffe brought the full force of a hammer down onto Jean's skull. He struck her again and again – eleven times in all. After pulling her body into some bushes, he was startled by the arrival of another car and made a fast getaway.

Known as 'Scotch Jean' to fellow sex workers, Jean had lived with her common-law husband, Alan Royle, and their two children in a Moss Side flat on Lingbeck Crescent, Hulme, about one mile south of the town. That day, Alan had gone out with friends, assuming that, when he returned home, Jean would be there. The children were asleep, but she wasn't at home.

For eight long days Sutcliffe waited for Jean's body to be discovered. He had realised that the £5 note he'd handed Jean before he killed her was one from his pay packet and a newly minted note. It could, if discovered by police, be a lead that would bring them straight to him. As the days went by, he decided to risk returning to Moss Side and Jean's body to find the note. During a frantic search, he could not find the woman's handbag and in an act of frustration he started to attack the body with a broken pane of glass. He even tried to cut off the head, thinking that this would remove his own tell-tale hammer blow signature. In the end he gave up, kicking the corpse several times before driving home.

One day later, an allotment owner found Jean's naked body and rang Chorlton-cum-Hardy police station. Jean's face was unrecognisable and there was no identifying evidence amongst her scattered clothing. She was eventually identified from a fingerprint on a lemonade bottle she had handled before leaving home for the last time.

The £5 note was found secreted away in a pocket in her bag and was a crucial clue. It had indeed come from Sutcliffe's wage packet which he had received two days earlier from T. & W.H. Clark where he worked. Within hours, Bank of England officials had established that the note, serial number AW51 121565, was part of a consignment sent to the Shipley and Bingley branches of the Midland Bank where staff were able to produce the names of 5,493 people who *could* have received the note as part of their wages. Sutcliffe was one of them.

A month after Jean Jordan's death, two officers knocked on Sutcliffe's door. They interviewed Sutcliffe twice but his alibi – that he had spent the evening of the murder at a family party – *seemed* genuine. In 1980, the £5 note clue was reinvestigated when a number of companies that might have put the note into an employee's wage packet were whittled down from thirty to just three, but Sutcliffe again escaped justice.

Marilyn Moore was twenty-five. She was attacked in Leeds on Wednesday, 14 December 1977. After agreeing to the customary £5 for short time sex with Sutcliffe, Marilyn allowed him to drive her to Scott Hall Street, on to Buslingthorpe Lane, heading for some waste ground some two hundred yards from the Prince Phillip Playing Fields where Sutcliffe had killed Wilma McCann over two years previously. When they parked, Sutcliffe suggested they have sex in the back seat of his car to which she agreed. The back passenger door was locked and when Sutcliffe came round to open it, he tried to hit her on the head with his hammer, but lost his balance slightly and caught her a glancing blow. She screamed loudly and held her head as she started to fall to the ground with him shouting: 'Dirty prostitute bitch,' hitting her eight times until she fell unconscious. Her screams and the barking of a dog quickly persuaded Sutcliffe to leave. When Marilyn regained consciousness, she staggered towards the road to get help and was rushed to Leeds Infirmary for emergency surgery, including relieving pressure on her brain from a depressed fracture of the skull. Marilyn had survived her encounter with the Yorkshire Ripper.

Yvonne Pearson was twenty-two and a sex worker who knew of the terrible dangers out there on those dark streets. She was murdered in Bradford on Saturday, 21 January 1978, her body not being found until two months later. Yvonne had left her two children, Colette and Lorraine, in the care of a sixteen-year-old neighbour before setting off for The Flying Dutchman pub at 9.30 p.m. Within minutes, she was seen climbing into a car driven by a bearded man with 'black, piercing eyes'.

On Easter Sunday, 26 March, a passerby walking down a street behind Silvio Bakery, close to White Abbey Road, saw an arm sticking out from under an old sofa, and a putrid smell assaulted his nose. He approached what, at first, he thought was a tailor's mannequin, he recognised that this was a body. The woman's head had been beaten until it was unrecognisable and her body was rotting.

In this incident Sutcliffe had a very narrow escape for as he was beating Maureen to death, a car with a couple inside, pulled up beside his car. He told police he took steps to make sure Maureen's moans didn't give him away.

'So, to stop the moaning I took some filling from the sofa. I held her nose and shoved the straw into her mouth, then I shoved it down her throat,' he told police. 'I let her go after a while to see if she was still making a noise, but when I did, she started again, so I pinched her nose again.

'When the car had gone I was seething with rage. Her jeans were nearly off, because she had undone them at the car, and when I was pulling her by the feet, I nearly pulled them off. I think I kicked her hard to the head and body. I was senseless with rage and I was kicking away furiously at her... after I killed her I apologised. I said I was sorry and she could get up, and that she would be all right. She didn't and I realise it was meant to be.'

And the murders continued. Helen Rytka was an eighteen-year-old sex worker who was murdered in Huddersfield, on Tuesday, 31 January 1978. She was a striking girl who always dreamed of owning her own home, however, by 31 January 1978, she was sharing a miserable room next to a motorway flyover in Huddersfield with her twin sister, Rita. Helen's life had started off like so many women who fall into sex work. Born to an Italian mother and a Jamaican father, she had spent most of her young life in care. Helen and Rita usually worked the streets as a pair to minimise the risk from men who might want to harm them. They would concentrate upon the limited red-light district in and around the depressed Great Northern Street area. The railway arches under the Leeds to Manchester line formed the brothels, but the twin sisters were above that. Rightfully wary of the danger following the previous Yorkshire Ripper murders, the girls had devised a system whereby they were picked up by clients at the same time outside a public lavatory. Each client would get the 'short time' of precisely twenty minutes, and the girls would return to the toilet to rendezvous. They even took the car registration number of each other's John before they set off.

For all of the girls' efforts to take precautions, it all went terrifyingly wrong on that snowy night. Helen arrived back at their meeting place five minutes early, at 9.25 p.m. A bearded man in a red Corsair offered her the chance of another quick £5.00, possibly even before Rita returned. The sisters never saw each other again.

Helen took the punter to nearby Garrard's Timber Yard, which straddles some railway arches. It was a popular haunt for women working on the streets. Unusually for him, Sutcliffe admitted that he had sexual intercourse with Helen but claimed it was only because of the presence of two men in the yard that forced him to delay his hammer attack. As a result, his £5 time limit was running out. He struck Helen as she climbed out of the back seat to return to the front seat, anxious no doubt to return to Rita. His first blow missed, striking the car door. His second blow found her head and then he hit her another five times. The attack was a few feet from the foreman's shed in the wood yard and so the walls were spattered with her blood.

Sutcliffe dragged Helen's body to a woodpile, where it was hidden. Her bra and black polo-neck sweater were found in the now characteristic position above her breasts and only her socks were left on. The rest of her clothing was scattered widely around the area. Her black lace underwear was found by a lorry driver on the site, pinned to a shed door. She had been horribly mutilated, with three stabs to the chest, and indications of repeated stabbings through the same wounds. There were also scratch marks on the chest. This wasn't just a case of overkill it was the work of a demon from Hell.

Vera Millward was forty-one. She was murdered in Manchester on Tuesday, 16 May 1978. Vera was a frail woman, who had endured three major operations, had chronic stomach issues and only one lung. She was the mother of seven and was a sex worker. Vera was killed in the well-lit grounds of the Manchester Royal Infirmary. Spanish-born Vera had arrived in the UK after the war as a home help. She soon resorted to prostitution in Manchester's Moss Side district to support her family.

On the night of her death, she told her Jamaican boyfriend that she was going out from their flat in Greenham Avenue, Hulme to buy cigarettes and get pain-killing drugs from the hospital to ease her chronic stomach pains. He knew she was really going out to try and earn some money on the street.

It was here that she encountered Peter Sutcliffe. After picking her up in his car, Sutcliffe hit her three times on the head with his hammer and then slashed her across the stomach. When a gardener spotted her body at 8.10 a.m. the next morning, on a rubbish pile, he at first thought that she was some sort of doll. Vera was lying on her right side, face down, her arms folded beneath her body and legs out straight. She was partly covered by a grey-coloured coat and a piece of paper was placed over her badly disfigured head.

'Before doing it, I had to go through a terrible stage each time. I was in absolute turmoil.'

Peter Sutcliffe

By the end of 1978, during a period of a little over twelve months, detectives had interviewed Sutcliffe no less than four times. He had been questioned twice about tyre treads that might match tracks identified at Irene Richardson's murder, twenty-one months earlier. Sutcliffe was always accommodating and unruffled. However, the officers were never asked to check his blood group (which was rare) or his shoe size (unusually small for a man) – at least two more of the firm facts known about this crazed homicidal monster.

Josephine Whitaker was aged nineteen when she was murdered in Halifax on Wednesday, 4 April 1979. Sutcliffe had driven from Bingley to Halifax. Just before midnight, he got out of his car and fell in step with Josephine as she walked across Savile Park playing fields. In his statements to police, he said that he spoke briefly to her, and then, as they moved away from the streetlamps, smashed the back of her skull with his hammer and dragged her into the shadows. Like something we might see in a horror film, this was, for Josephine, a dread nightmare come true.

Josephine's body was found early the next morning. Like Jayne MacDonald, she had no links to sex work, lived at home with her parents and worked as a clerk at the headquarters of the Halifax Building Society. Police had, up until now, thought that they were dealing with a killer who was targeting sex workers only. But with Jayne and Josephine now dead, it was clear that no woman was safe. Any woman who had the nerve to walk the streets at night was at risk. From that moment on and overnight all women in the north of England lost their liberty. And here we find another issue to resolve, for Josephine's murder had allegedly not only changed the way the police approached the investigation but it was also used at trial to prove that Sutcliffe had a sexual motivation for his murders – a screwdriver had been inserted into her, thus, police reasoned that it wasn't Sutcliffe's 'mission to destroy prostitutes' as he had claimed.

As we all should know, the Ripper investigation was one almighty botch-up from start to end, thus I disagree entirely with the police's sudden sea-change regarding Sutcliffe's prime motive being sexual. That this beast had inserted a screwdriver into the poor girl, I am almost mortified to say, is highly-indicative of his utter hatred for women and his need to violate them in the most disgusting way possible.

Barbara Leach was a twenty-year-old student in her second year at Bradford University, working towards a degree in social psychology. She was murdered during a late night walk in Bradford after a night with friends. Sutcliffe was cruising the streets around Little Horton – a residential area for many students which again was not part of the red-light district. It was just after 1 a.m. on Sunday, 2 September 1979 when he spotted Barbara moving away from a group of friends outside the 'Mannville Arms' on Great Horton Road.

Sutcliffe struck with his hammer in Ash Grove, just 200 yards from the pub and then dragged Barbara into the shadows of somebody's backyard, where he stabbed her eight times before putting her body into a dustbin recess and slinging an old carpet over it. Her body was not found until late the following afternoon.

By now, Peter Sutcliffe had been interviewed by police no less than nine times and was still killing. But, as the fear and fervour grew around the Ripper killings and the police investigation came under more pressure to make an arrest, it would be almost a year before he would kill again.

Marguerite Walls was forty-seven and a civil servant at the Department of Education and Science. She had been working overtime in her office in Pudsey on the night of 20 August 1980. She was about to go on leave for ten days and wanted to tidy her desk. She left her office between 9.30 and 10.30 p.m. and began the half mile walk to her home in Farsley.

Sutcliffe was on his way to Chapeltown and driving through Farsley when he spotted Marguerite. She was his twelfth victim. Two days later, her body was found, buried under a mound of grass clippings in the wooded grounds of a magistrate's home. She had been bludgeoned and strangled. As the result of an apparently different MO, police initially refused to include this homicide in the Ripper sequence. If Sutcliffe had changed his MO in a deliberate effort to convince the police that the Ripper killings were over, then it worked. But Sutcliffe couldn't stop.

*

He attacked thirty-four-year-old, Dr. Upadhya Bandra in Leeds, on Wednesday, 24 September 1980. She was visiting the city to attend a course at the Nuffield centre. Sutcliffe hit her over the head and again used a ligature to try and strangle her. A local woman came to investigate a noise and subsequently called the police as Sutcliffe fled. Dr. Bandra survived.

Theresa Sykes was sixteen when she was attacked in Huddersfield on the night of Wednesday, 5 November

1980. She was on her way back from the grocery store and was almost home when Sutcliffe emerged from the darkness and struck her from behind. Neighbours, her boyfriend and her father heard her screams and came to her aid. Sutcliffe fled and hid under a hedge for some time before they gave up the search for Theresa's attacker. It was the closest he'd come to being caught in the act. Theresa was able to give a description of the man to police, however, once again the attack was not linked to the Ripper series initially but later would prove crucial in identifying Sutcliffe as his later alibi for this attack fell apart. But Sutcliffe would have the chance to steal one last life.

Jaqueline Hill was twenty and a student in her third year studying for a degree in English. She was murdered in Leeds on Monday, 17 November 1980. She was the Ripper's final victim. Jacqueline alighted a bus in Otley Road, opposite the local Kentucky Fried Chicken shack, and she was in sight of Lupton Flats – a hall of residence – when Sutcliffe, his fingers still greasy from his KFC supper, brutally struck her down. He dragged her onto wasteland behind the parade of shops and fell upon her with manic frenzy. Death had struck this dear lass so suddenly that one of her eyes remained open. After dragging her around thirty yards to some wasteland behind the Arndale centre, he stabbed repeatedly at her chest and once at the sightless eye with a rusting Phillips screwdriver.

Peter Sutcliffe was arrested by Sergeant Robert 'Bob' Ring and PC Robert Hydes as they started their evening shift. They were cruising along Melbourne Avenue in Sheffield – a regular haunt of sex workers and their clients – when they saw Olivia Reivers climbing into a Rover V8 3500. It was a toss of a coin whether they would bother to investigate alleged soliciting, nevertheless, they took a stroll over.

The driver identified himself as Peter Williams and said that the car was his own. He wanted no trouble. Scrambling out, he asked immediately if he could relieve himself. Sergeant Ring nodded in good-tempered exasperation, and the small, bearded man sidled over to the shadowy bushes lining the grubby lane. Under the cover of darkness, he removed a ball-peen hammer and a sharpened knife from a special pocket in his car coat, and hid them. Mouthy Olivia, remonstrated with the cops, but had no idea that she was abusing the men who had just saved her life.

By the time 'Mr Williams' walked back to his car, the police had established that his number plates were false and both Olivia and her client were taken to Hammerton Road Police Station for further questioning. Sutcliffe would never be a free man again.

The question now remains, if a similar killer with a similar MO were to stalk the red-light districts of the UK again, would he be caught more quickly? In all likelihood the answer is 'yes'! These days we have CCTV, mobile phone tracking, and state-of-the-art technology that 'The Ripper Squad' could never have dreamed of.

Aged seventy-four, Peter Sutcliffe died of natural causes at HMP Full Sutton, Friday, 13 November 2020. Let him burn in Hell.

★★★

Richard Benjamin Speck

'When someone is going through a storm, a nurse's
presence is more powerful than a million empty words.'

Medelita

This chapter on Richard Speck, like all that preceded it
and those to follow, is not intended to be an exhaustive
account of an offender's narrative – far from it – for the
reader may well wish to carry out even more research
on any offender piquing one's interest. There is ample
reference material to be found in books, magazines, and
online. As I stated from the outset, this book is really about
why I believe that these killers deserve a special place in
Hell, that is my purpose here, nothing more, nothing less.

As my loyal readers know all too well, I thoroughly
enjoy wandering off into the realms of black humour and
often write with a modicum of irreverent levity thrown
in for good measure. And why not? Murder most foul
is a disgustingly evil state-of-affairs so one has to lighten
the load occasionally. This is especially true when we're
dealing with the worst of the Devil's spawn, and Mr
Richard Speck is one of the very worst. And he's our next

prime candidate for a very, *very* special place, in Hell. But there will be no dark humour or levity in this chapter – well maybe a little then – I can assure the reader of this. What Speck did, which I find particularly upsetting today, is that he raped and murdered eight student nurses from the South Chicago Community Hospital during the night of Wednesday, 13 July 1966, and into the early hours of the following day.

A record seventy-two people were murdered in 'The Windy City' in 1966. It had been a blistering summer and, as we all know, so much stifling heat can inflame tempers. Just the day before the nurses were killed, a minor incident sparked a criminal wildfire in the form of the Chicago West Side riots which raged from July 12 to 15. An ex-convict named William Young, who was wanted for armed robbery, attempted to evade arrest at a liquor store on the 100 block of South Pulaski Road. Young fled from CPD officers Biaggio Panepinto and James Rizzi and began screaming that the officers were trying to kill him, attracting a crowd of around two hundred. The mob surrounded the cops, demanding they release Young. The officers were eventually rescued by colleagues, but now the troublemakers began to loot the liquor store starting the unrest on the West Side. The riots reached their height on 14 July when 1,200 National Guardsmen were called in to restore order. Following an appeal by Civil Rights leader, Dr. Martin Luther King, the violence began to wind down. Nevertheless, hundreds of stores were looted during the riots; two black men were killed by stray sniper fire and police arrested more than two hundred people.

As this unrest in Chicago rumbled on, the events of the night of the 13 July would shake the world to its core. The night's death toll would exceed the Chicago St Valentine's Day Massacre of six gangsters on 14 February 1929. Hardened mobsters blasting each other away is all well and good – the jolly mutual destruction of an obnoxious species, we might say. But that night saw the slaughtering of 'Angels of Mercy', and it was something much darker for anyone who kills a nurse certainly deserves a place in Hell. Furthermore, as I write this chapter, we are in the midst of the COVID-19 pandemic. Tens-of-thousands of doctors, nurses and frontliners are risking their lives every hour of every day across the world, and some are dying as the result. These compassionate, selfless, loving professionals are people we should honour greatly. Richard Speck did not.

It was a sultry night in the city with thunder clouds rolling in off Lake Michigan, lowering the temperature a few degrees, but increasing the humidity. Jeffery Manor was one of many new suburbs that had been developed after World War Two to help accommodate Chicago's growing population. By 1966, 'The Manor' had grown into a largely middle-class neighbourhood of Georgian-style houses, neat terraces and wide lawns that hosted a large Jewish community. Despite the number of unemployed seamen in the area, seeking work at nearby Calument Harbor, crime was rare with most police time being devoted to petty crime, such as cycle theft. But a singular event was going to turn everything upside down.

In a two-storey townhouse at 2319 East 100th Street, the windows were open to welcome any respite to the sticky night air. The reader can easily find this address by searching Google Maps, and when one hears the story of what happened that night, one might be surprised to learn that the house *remains exactly the same* today as it did in the sixties. Number 2319 is one of six identical modern buildings in the block between Luella and Crandon Avenues. Three of these buildings were hospital hostels where nurses lived, eight women to each house. Living in 2319 were Corazon Amurao (twenty-three) and Valentina Pasion (twenty-three) both from the Philippines as well as fellow Filipina Merlita Gargullo (twenty-two) from Santa Cruz who had been in Chicago for only a month. Their American dorm sisters were Patricia Matusek (twenty) who was the daughter of a liquor salesman; Pamela Wilkening (twenty) from Lansing, Illinois who had always wanted to be a nurse; Nina Jo Schmale (twenty-four) who was a one-time Sunday school teacher from Wheaton; Gloria Davy (twenty-two) from Dyer, Indiana, where her father worked in a steel mill and Suzanne Farris (twenty-one) who was engaged to Mary Ann Jordan's brother. That July evening, Suzanne and Gloria were out – Gloria was with her boyfriend. But let's leave this scene whilst there is still peace and calm and return to an earlier time to explore the monster that would shatter these young women's lives.

'BORN TO RAISE HELL'
Tattoo on Speck's left arm below the elbow

There is little to say about Kirkwood (formerly Lyndon), Illinois, apart from the fact that it was renamed in May 1874, in honour of the former governor of Iowa, Samuel J. Kirkwood for reasons unknown – he never visited Kirkwood *or* parked his horse there, and he ain't buried there either. He rests in Oakland Cemetery, Iowa City. It is not unsurprising to learn that as it only sits on about

0.92 sq miles, Kirkwood only has a few notable residents. Captain Louis A. Kaiser, a pioneer in the Navy on the use of wireless telegraphy who was *briefly* in charge of the government on Guam prior to World War One. Worth Ryder, was an artist, curator and art professor who was largely responsible for the United States early interest in avant-garde art. And then there is Richard Speck.

Richard Benjamin Speck – sometimes erroneously called Richard *Franklin* Speck – was born on Monday, 6 September 1941, in Kirkwood which then had a population of around 650. Speck was the seventh of eight siblings born to Benjamin Franklin Speck, a packer at a local pottery, and his wife Mary Margaret Carbaugh. By the end of 1947, Speck Sr. had died from a heart attack. Richard, a boy who was close to his father, was just six years old.

In 1950, Speck's teetotaller religious mother married a twenty-five-year-old travelling insurance salesman named Carl August Randolph Lindbergh whom she met on a train bound for Chicago. He was a drinker and had a twenty-five-year criminal record ranging from forgery to drunk driving. Mary's two youngest children, Richard and Carolyn, took their stepfather's name and the four of them moved to Santo, 40 miles west of Fort Worth, Dallas, Texas.

Richard hated his stepfather who was the polar opposite of his father, and family arguments would sometimes end in fisticuffs. He suffered quite a lot of psychological abuse and started drinking aged twelve. His first arrest, in 1955, aged thirteen for trespassing, was followed by dozens of other misdemeanours over the following eight years.

By the age of fifteen he was getting drunk almost every day and a teacher at his junior high school remembered that 'he seemed lost. It didn't seem like he knew what was going on. I wasn't able to teach him anything. I don't think I ever saw him smile. No one could get through to him. He was a loner. He seemed so sulky. He didn't have any friends in class.' Speck then went on to attend a Technical High School, but quit after just one term.

Speck's problems seem to have stemmed from a catalogue of head injuries that started aged five. Some say that he accidentally hit himself with a claw hammer while playing in a sandbox. Why any mother would leave such a dangerous item laying around a kid of that age, beats me, but perhaps the truth is that it came about during a fight with his stepfather, but in the woolly theme of things let's leave it that he got hit with a hammer. Aged ten, he fell headlong from a tree, and was unconscious for ninety minutes. The following year, he ran headlong into a steel rod supporting a shop awning and had a bicycle accident with both incidents rendering him temporarily unconscious. To this can be added injuries he received in innumerable fights. He was hit seven or eight times over the skull with a tyre iron in a bungled robbery attempt. His headaches and blackouts began a year after he was clubbed by a Dallas cop. In addition to this, when three months old and suffering from pneumonia, blood supplies to his brain were blocked. He had sunstroke after picking cotton at a Texas prison farm. And, of course, he became a hardened alcoholic. To say that Richard Speck was born on the wrong side of tracks and was psychologically and physically screwed from pretty much the get-go would be the understatement of the century.

To try and thread our way through Speck's narrative a little more, we know that between 1960 and 1963 he worked as a labourer for the 7-Up bottling company in Dallas, during which time he met cute, gingham-skirt-and-pop-sox-wearing fifteen-year-old Shirley Annette Malone at the Texas State Fair. Within three weeks she was pregnant. They married on 19 January 1962 and she moved in with him, his mother, sister Carolyn, and Carolyn's husband. When their daughter, Robbie Lynn Speck, was born on 5 July 1962, little did his Shirley know that Richard was a serving a twenty-two-day jail sentence for disturbing the peace in McKinney, Texas, and getting into a drunken melee.

In July 1963, he was caught after he forged and cashed a co-worker's $44 paycheck. He robbed a grocery store, making away with cigarettes, beer and a measly $3 in cash. Now twenty-one, he was convicted of forgery and burglary and sentenced to three years in prison. He was paroled after serving sixteen months from 1963 to 1965 in the Texas State Penitentiary aka 'The Walls' Huntsville – which also houses the death house and it seems a great pity that he wasn't executed there and then for his problems with the law had merely started.

One week after being placed on parole, on 9 January 1965, wielding a seventeen-inch carving knife, he attacked a woman in the parking lot of her apartment building. She screamed and he was arrested within minutes to be awarded a sixteen-month sentence for aggravated assault to run concurrently with a parole violation sentence, and returned to the pen.

By now the reader will be asking, 'What the fuck is wrong with this man?' And, you'd be correct to enquire for due to a cock-up in the prison system, he was released six months early. For three months he worked for the Patterson Meat Company as a driver. Did they check for any references, no they didn't, however, he repaid them by having six – yes six – accidents with his truck before the firm woke up and fired him.

In December 1965 he moved in with a twenty-nine-year-old divorcee – and a former professional wrestler come to that – and a bartender at his favourite bar, 'Ginny's Lounge' – a clip joint populated almost entirely by 'hooks' aka petty criminals, toughs and sundry unsavoury folk, and where naïve folk pay ridiculous tabs for watered-down booze and cheap thrills.

Since the days of legendary local gangsters Delois Green and Herbert Noble, Dallas has always had a reputation for tough, mean bars, and Ginny's was one of them. And, we must remember that Dallas began as a swashbuckling, gambling-a-whoring frontier town and that legacy has never left Texas blood and a lot of blood has been and still is spilt on those sawdust strewn floors. As one local told me and my TV producer, Frazer, when we visited Dallas/Fort Worth: 'When we say these places are mean, we aren't kidding. We're talking about bars where you literally take your life in your hands when you walk in the door.' Yes, folks, tis so true, so me and Frazer opted for something more convivial – a pole-dancing club called 'The Two Minnies' out on the beltway, and we sat as close to the door as one could ☺.

But I have digressed again, so back to Richard and his lady wrestler who was amply qualified to deal with troublesome drinkers with her arm wrenches, double underhooks, a suplex, a DDT, a face-buster or a powerbomb; well, she did have three kids and needed a babysitter, and that's the reason he moved in with her.

In January 1966, sweet little Carolyn filed for divorce, and that same month, Speck stabbed a customer in a knife fight in 'Ginny's Lounge'. His mom came to the rescue towing an attorney who was able to get the charge reduced to disturbing the peace. Speck was fined $10 and jailed for three days after he failed to pay the fine.

'Enough already, please Christopher,' I hear you plead, but we have to learn that on 5 March 1966 he bought a twelve-year-old car; the following evening he robbed a grocery store and stole seventy cartons of ciggies. Now sit down and take a stiff drink because this will take some swallowing. He sold the nicked cigarettes out of the trunk of his car in the store's parking lot and then abandoned the car. I mean one could not make this up if one tried. Quite obviously, police soon tracked him down but Richard had no intention hanging around, for his arrest (his forty-second in Dallas) would mean another spell behind bars, so his sister drove him to the bus depot where he hopped onto the Greyhound bound for Chicago, Illinois.

It is almost unbearable for me to go on and on about this man's further antecedents, but in brief he was continually in trouble. On one occasion he threatened a man with a knife in a restroom. At 1 a.m. on 3 April, sixty-five-year-old Mrs Virgil Harris returned to her home from babysitting to find a burglar brandishing a knife. Speck tied her up, raped her, ransacked the house and stole her $2.50 babysitting money.

A week later, thirty-two-year-old barmaid, Mary Kathryn Pierce, went missing. Her body was found inside an empty hog house on 13 April behind 'Frank's

Place'; a Monmouth tavern owned by her brother-in-law and where she worked. She had died from a blow to her abdomen that ruptured her liver.

Now having finally washed up in Chicago at the beginning of July, at first, he stayed with his married sister, Martha Thornton, who lived in a second-floor apartment at 3966 N. Avondale Avenue, in the old Irving Park neighbourhood, Northwest Side of 'The Windy City' while he looked for work.

Pretty soon, his pale, pockmarked face with its hollow cheeks and high cheekbones became a common sight in Chicago's sleazier taverns. His watery-blue eyes were often clouded by drugs – barbiturates were his favourite, though he would try anything on offer – and his big, bucket-shaped hands were usually grasping a glass. He looked like a ghoul and certainly not someone you would want to find unannounced at your bedroom door in the dead of night.

Every day, though, he checked in at the seaman's union to see if there was a ship needing crew, so on 25 April Speck went to the US Coast Guard office and applied for a letter of authority to work as an apprentice seaman. This application required being fingerprinted and photographed, and having a physical examination by a doctor. With the great gift of hindsight, perhaps a criminal record check might have been conducted by the US Coast Guard; as for the physical examination, what more can one say? Even a blind vet would have realised that Speck was a mental and physical car wreck, as his next employers soon would discover.

Speck immediately joined the crew of Inland Steel's *Clarence B. Randall*, an L6-S-B1 class bulk ore lake freighter. The voyage was brief. On 3 May he was evacuated by the very same authority who had rubber-stamped him as being fit and well – airlifted by helicopter to hospital where he underwent an emergency appendectomy. After he recovered, on 20 May, he rejoined the same vessel on which he served until 14 June, when he got drunk and argued with one of the ship's officers and was put ashore. The calendar was now turning pages towards the date of the most horrific act of mass murder in Chicago's history.

On 30 June, he visited the National Maritime Union (NMU) hiring hall at 3225 E. 100th Street, to file his paperwork for a seaman's card. The place was just one block east from where the exchange nurses lived; eight of whom lived in the easternmost townhouse at 2310 E. 100th Street – just 150 feet from the NMU hall.

On Friday, 8 July, Speck registered for a berth on the SS *Flying Spray*, a C1-A cargo ship bound for South Vietnam, but his luck was out for a seaman with more seniority got the berth.

When he got wind of a job on an Indiana ore-carrier, on Tuesday 12 July, and having by now been thrown out of his sister's house, he quit his rented room, and received an offer of an assignment on Sinclair Oil's tanker, SS *Sinclair Great Lakes*. But now fate played a deadly hand in the form of the Major Arcana card which typically depicts the 'Grim Reaper'. When Speck arrived at the dock, he was told there had been a mix-up. Someone else had been given the job. Penniless and dejected, and now with nowhere to stay, he left his bags at a Shell gas station near the NMU hiring hall and went on a drinking spree before spending the night in a half-finished house just off E. 103rd Street.

The next morning, however, he awoke holding 'The Ace of Pentacles' – in Tarot this means material abundance, wealth, money and opportunity. Speck was offered a job on an ocean-going ship sailing the following Monday. Excitedly, he phoned his brother-in-law, who brought him $25 to keep him going until he sailed. Speck took a room at the Shipyard Inn, a seedy hotel on Chicago's South Side, and went to play pool. A good player, he won some more money. Things were now really looking up. He took six 'redbirds' – barbiturate pills – and went for a stroll by Lake Michigan.

'It was just one of them weird coincidences. I was high on heroin that night. Heroin and whisky. I'd never shot heroin before. So eight people got killed.'
Richard Speck quoted in the Chicago Tribune,
8 December 1991

Speck had, in fact, never shot heroin but he had been on the drink since he'd opened his eyes that morning, and the combo of booze and pills filled him with a warm glow. About 3 p.m. he was back in the bars where he fell into conversation with three men who said that they were sailors.

'Yeah, I killed them, I stabbed them and I choked them. If that one girl wouldn't have spit in my face, they'd all be alive today. It ain't like on TV… it takes over three minutes and you have to have a lot of strength.'
Richard Speck speaking to the Chicago Tribune,
8 December 1991

At 11 p.m. on the night of 14 July, Corazon Amurao had just settled down to sleep in the upstairs room she shared with her colleague, Merlita Gargullo, when she heard four soft knocks at the bedroom door. Thinking that it was one of the other nurses, Corazon unlocked the door. A tall young man with a soft, gentle eyes pushed his way into the room. He was swaying slightly, and reeked of alcohol. He had a gun in his hand. 'I'm not going to hurt you,' he reassured her in a soft drawl, 'I need your money to go to New Orleans.' Corazon knew she had no choice but to obey.

The man ushered Corazon, Merlita and Valentina into the next room which Patricia, Pamela and Nina Jo shared. He made them sit on the floor and asked them where they kept their money. One by one, the women fetched their purses. The haul did not amount to much – certainly less than $100. All the while Speck insisted he had no intention of harming anyone.

At 11.30 p.m., another of the girls, Gloria Davy, returned from her date, and Speck met her as she came into the bedroom. He relieved her of the $2 she had. Then he cut a bedsheet into strips with a small pocketknife and tied up all of the women by their wrists.

Speck had no intention of leaving for he knew that the nurses would be able to describe him to police, so he hunkered down besides his captives and chatted to them, all the while tapping his gun barrel on the floor. He was showing signs of anxiety – frequently looking out of the bedroom window. Speck was not even a moderately intelligent man at his best, and now he was befuddled with booze and half-stoned with the pills and the injected liquid, sex came into his mind. He led Pam Wilkening from the room. Shortly, thereafter, those left behind heard a deep sigh, and then silence. The Biography Channel suggests that Speck tried to rape Pamela but she was defiant so he killed her, however, be that as it may, she died at his hands whatever the scenario.

Suzanne Farris arrived home around midnight. She brought back a friend, another student nurse, Mary Ann Jordan. As they did so, Speck walked in behind them, brandishing his gun, and ushered them out again. The remaining nurses heard a commotion and muffled shouts then silence, broken by the sound of running water in the bathroom.

After about twenty minutes, Speck returned for another nurse, Nina Schmale. By this time, his remaining captives were terrified. Corazon Amurao quietly rolled herself across the floor and wriggled under one of the two-tier bunk beds. The next time Speck came back, it was to remove Merlita Gargullo and Valentina Pasion. From her hiding place, Corazon heard both girls 'grunt'. Merlita called out, 'It hurts', in her native Tagalog before the heavy silence descended again. Corazon lay stock still.

The next nurse to leave the room was Patricia Matusek. Speck bent down and carried her away. As she went, Corazon heard her ask, 'Will you please untie my ankles first?' Amurao and Gloria Davy were the only ones left in the room. The young Filipino crushed herself even tighter under the gap under the bed. After what had become a standard twenty-five-minute pause, Corazon heard the man come back. She saw him removing Gloria's jeans, unzip his own black trousers, and climb on top of her. Corazon looked away, but the rhythmic creaking of the bedsprings told her what was happening. At one point she heard the intruder ask, in the same disconcerting gentle voice, 'Will you please put your legs around my back?' Then the creaking stopped.

The house was now as silent as the grave. Corazon lay petrified in her cramped hiding place, afraid to move or make a sound. At 5.00 a.m. an alarm clock went off in one of the other bedrooms. The girls usually left for work at 6.30 a.m. to start their shifts at the hospital.

At 6 a.m., Corazon managed to free herself of her bonds. Fearfully, she inched her way down the hall to her own bedroom, where she found the bodies of Mary Ann Jordan, Suzanne Farris and Pamela Wilkening. There was blood everywhere. Corazon dashed to her bedroom window and crawled out onto a ledge that fronted the property, ten-foot above ground level. Crouching there, passersby heard her screaming, 'They are all dead. My friends are all dead. Oh God, I'm the only one alive.'

Daniel Kelly was the first cop to arrive. He had been cruising the local streets in his squad car. He found that the rear door to the house was swinging open; a panel had been forced out. He entered. In the living room he found the naked body of a young woman with a piece of cloth tied tightly around her neck. Turning her over, he immediately recognised her as Gloria Davy – Charlene Davy, Gloria's sister, had once been his girlfriend.

There were seven more bodies upstairs. Patricia Matusek was in the bathroom. She had been kicked in the stomach then strangled. In a heap on the floor in the westernmost of the two front bedrooms lay Merlita Gargullo and Valentina Pasion. Nina Schmale was on one of the beds. All the women had been stabbed in the neck. Miss Gargullo and Miss Schmale had also been strangled.

Lying on the floor of the front east bedroom were Mary Ann Jordan and Suzanne Farris. Both had been stabbed several times before being strangled. Farris, who had apparently put up a fight, had been wounded eighteen times. On one of the beds lay Pamela Wilkening, who had a stab wound in her breast and a strip of cloth wound around her neck.

'There has never been anything like it that I have heard. It is the crime of the century. It is the worst crime I have even seen.'
Andrew Toman, Cook County Coroner to reporters

The police gently coaxed the distraught Corazon out of the house of horrors and took her to the South Community Hospital, where she was sedated. She was able to give police a detailed description of that nightmarish night though and also the man who had killed her friends. She told them about his distinctive tattoo that read 'BORN TO RAISE HELL.'

There was no shortage of clues for the CSI's to find in the house on East Street. Latent fingerprints and palm prints were lifted from the doors, walls and furniture. Police found a man's T-shirt, soaked in sweat in the living room and another was found wrapped in Gloria Davy's jeans.

Very quickly, cops discovered that a man answering Corazon's description of the killer had left his bags at a gas station just across the road from the murder house on the Tuesday night. He had told the attendant he was looking for a job on a ship, which narrowed things down considerably. The branch office of the NMU was a few yards away and here police learned that someone had called by the previous day looking for a berth on a ship that was bound for New Orleans. By luck, in a wastepaper basket investigators found a crumpled application form with the name Richard Benjamin Speck at the top.

Little more needs to be said as to how police finally tracked Speck down, needless to say that after a half-hearted attempt at committing suicide he was arrested at midnight at Cook County Hospital at midnight, Sunday, 17 July 1966, after a doctor recognised Speck's 'BORN TO RAISE HELL' tattoo.

> 'I had no feelings at all that night. They said there was blood all over the place. I can't remember. It felt like nothing. You know why those cunts died? Because it just wasn't their fucking night.'
> *Richard Speck quoted in the* Chicago Tribune,
> *8 December 1991*

On Tuesday, 26 July 1966, Speck was indicted on eight counts of first-degree murder. His trial opened in the small town of Peoria on Monday, 20 February 1967. He was sentenced to death on Monday, 6 June that year. Unfazed by the verdict, he told reporters, 'If I burn, I burn.' The death sentence was later overturned, and on Wednesday, 22 November 1972, he was re-sentenced to 400-1,200 years imprisonment.

If there is anything in this dreadful case that can even begin to ease the enormity of it all, it is the way the surviving witness, Corazon Amurao, handled herself throughout her terrifying ordeal.

Corazon was born and raised in San Luis, Batangas Province. A dark-haired beauty, she qualified as a nurse in Manila and went to the US for further training at the start of June 1966, when she was twenty-three years old. Corazon had scrimped and saved every peso she could to pay for her trip. Nurses in the Philippines – even as I write this today – are only paid around 400 pesos (£6.50) per day, and out of this they have to pay for their own food and travel expenses.

Physically tiny at just four foot ten inches tall, Corazon proved mentally tough. She was largely responsible for the identification and subsequent conviction of Richard Speck. Although, as might be expected, her testimony was punctuated by tears and sobs, one observer described her as: 'the perfect prosecution witness,' businesslike with the facts, but not cold and dehumanised with their personal implications, with perhaps the most dramatic moment when she pointed directly at Speck and identified him as the monster who had killed her colleagues. After the trial, Corazon Amurao returned to her nursing career. I urge you to look her up online and read more of her story – box of tissues at the ready, please.

Speck died in prison of a heart attack on 5 December 1991, the eve of his fiftieth birthday. All that is left for me to add is that – as he was so proud of his 'BORN TO RAISE HELL' tattoo – I award him a very special place there.

★★★

Allen 'Tiny' Lee Davis

All killers of children rightly deserve a special place in Hell. We can include amongst them the British killer couples, Myra Hindley and Ian Brady, and Rose and Fred West. We might even include Jon Venables and Robert Thompson who became the youngest convicted murderers in England after killing two-year-old James Patrick Bulger in 1993. These juvenile monsters abducted the toddler from a Bootle shopping mall in Merseyside, and took him to a disused railway line, where they tortured and beat him to death. Actually, Venables isn't in Hell just yet – he is roaming through society today. As is Colin Pitchfork, the first person in criminal history to have been convicted of double homicide based on DNA screening. This sexual psychopath killed Lynda Rosemarie Mann (murdered November 1983) and Dawn Amanda Ashworth (murdered July 1986) both aged fifteen, in the Leicester villages of Narborough and Enderby respectively. He was arrested on 19 September 1987 and sentenced to life imprisonment on 22 January 1988. He isn't in Hell yet, either, so take a guess where he is? Go on. Please give it your best shot.

The answer is – wait for it... in Bristol, where he swans around as smug as fuck on unsupervised day release from his open prison all at the taxpayer's expense. What should have been provided *free* to Pitchfork was a hempen rope, if you care to ask me. But, no. There he is, pictured in a few tabloids wearing his top-of-the-range running shoes, while his two victims are buried deep in their graves, their parents' lives ruined forever. Dawn is buried at St John The Baptist Churchyard, Enderby, while Lynda rests in Narborough Cemetery. Sexual psychopaths are incurable – they will *always* remain an extreme danger to the public, so what kind of psychiatric lunacy allowed this man even an inch of freedom? Lord only knows!

Who can forget Ian Kevin Huntley who committed the murders of two ten-year-olds in Soham, Cambridgeshire, on 4 August 2002? Holly Marie Wells and Jessica Aimee Chapman were likely killed by asphyxiation. Their bodies were disposed of in an irrigation ditch close to RAF Lakenheath, Suffolk. Huntley's then girlfriend, Maxine Ann Carr, a teaching assistant who taught Holly and Jessica, provided Huntley with a false alibi. She received a three-and-a-half-year prison term for conspiring with Huntley to pervert the course of justice. He is now serving his life tariff at HMP Full Sutton, York. At the time of writing, Huntley, is forty-six years old and is always complaining about his civil rights being breached, probably whining to other resident monsters such as: John David Guise Cannan, John Duffy and the rest of the scum enjoying *free* food, *free* TV, *free* medical care and dental treatment and being addressed by prison staff as 'Sir' or 'Mr So-and-So'.

But now, let's return to the subject of this chapter, one not so tiny Mr Allen 'Tiny' Lee Davis (1944–1999). I have not just picked his name out of a hat for the grim sake of it. My reasons why will soon become gruesomely apparent; Our Lord put a bloody mark on this killer's chest as Davis burned alive in Florida's three-legged 'Yellow Mamma' and for a damned good reason too.

Davis, who came to be known as prisoner FDC #040174, was five foot and ten inches, with greying to white hair and hazel eyes. He was born 20 July 1944. He was known as Tiny but small he certainly wasn't. He weighed 350 pounds at the time of his execution for mass murder. He was convicted of killing Nancy Weiler who at the time was three months pregnant on 11 May 1982. Nancy was a Westinghouse executive's wife in the upscale – as our US cousins call a 'posh place' – area of Jacksonville. She was hit twenty-five times in her face and head and 'beaten almost beyond recognition,' with a .375 Magnum revolver taken from Davis's stepfather's house. Her nine-year-old daughter, Kristina, was tied up, raped, and shot twice in the face. Five-year-old daughter, Katherine, was shot as she tried to run away and then her skull was beaten in with the gun. Davis stole a Nikon camera from the house.

Davis later confessed to his attorney, Frank Tassone, about this grizzly homicide: 'She [Nancy] was bound with her hands behind her back, then she was hit with the barrel of the gun, maybe the grips of the gun, and I shot her. There was considerable crying and screaming by the children.'

The mental evaluation and diagnosis were that Davis was an: 'antisocial personality', and that he also had a psychosexual disorder and was a paedophile. However, Dr. Miller's opinion was that 'the crime was not the product of insanity but instead was the product of Davis's desire for money; he had chosen the place he did because it looked like a good place to rob.' But, for the record, it's best that the reader understands that 'Tiny' had some history, and none of it is very nice.

Davis had robbed an oil company employee at gunpoint. He'd once destroyed some machinery at work in a fit of anger, and in an unrelated episode he had deliberately driven another motorist off the road. This almost sub-human had a list of antecedents as long as his arm.

As all of my loyal readers know well, I am no 'Bible Thumper', no 'Preacher Man' either, although I do own several Holy Bibles, one placed by 'Gideons' in a Manila hotel which I mysteriously found in my suitcase when I unpacked in Dubai. Must have been God's will, and there are two sides to the capital punishment debate: those who support it and those against. I'd put money on it that Nancy's husband, John, couldn't have given a damn whether or not Davis was of unsound mind. This killer's appeals against the death sentence, costing millions of dollars, all the way up to Florida's Supreme Court were an additional insult to injury. I am certain that John would be very comfortable that Davis suffered an agonising death in the hot seat.

It is true that there have been some awful miscarriages of justice over the decades with innocent people being executed for crimes they did not commit. It is also true to say that it has been proven that the threat of capital punishment does not deter most dreadful homicides from taking place. However, I am minded to recall what His Honour, Judge Stuart Namm along with His Honour, Judge Stark from Long Island told me years ago. 'Society makes the rules. We all must live within those rules or anarchy reigns supreme. If someone decides to break the rules, then that is their decision. In an aggravated murder case, where the death penalty is applicable, the offender spits into the face of society knowing all too well of the possible consequences. Effectively, he, or she, hangs themselves, we merely provide the rope.'

It can be argued that execution is barbaric. It is not something that a 'civilised society' should tolerate. In the US it can be construed as a 'cruel or unusual punishment' or a bloodthirsty revenge. Of course, this is all well and good until one of the anti-death penalty lobby tragically has their own dearly beloved robbed, tortured and slain. Then they might adopt a different attitude altogether.

In Leviticus 42, 17–21, 'Lev' quotes the Lord instructing Moses in words that uphold the death penalty and includes the phrase: 'If anyone injures his neighbour, whatever he has done must be done to him: fracture for fracture, eye for eye, tooth for tooth.' Indeed, Mr Deuteronomy 19–21 somewhat plagiarised this with: 'Life for life, eye for eye, tooth for tooth, hand for hand, foot for foot.' I like that. Don't you?

When we reflect on all of the monsters featuring thus far in this book, and let's focus in again on Allen Lee Davis, for we might be obliged to ask ourselves did Nancy and her young kiddies get a chance to appeal to Davis as he terrified the wits out of them and suffered upon them the most heinous of deaths? Of course not!

If that had been *my* wife and children he had murdered, then I would have been the first in line to have pulled the switch. Would not you?

It might have been by chance or by design, but Davis's execution did not go smoothly. Perhaps the executioners purposely 'botched' the job when it came down to frying Tiny in Old Sparky. Pitiful and clinically obese, he was taken to the chair in a wheelchair, almost certainly shitting the proverbial bricks. Those who watched the execution, including a number of journalists whom I have met over the years, say that the mouth strap was pulled so tightly he moaned that he couldn't breathe because not only did it cover his mouth it pinched his nose too tight. He was suffocating. There can be no doubt that the chair was in disrepair, either. Something went wrong because during his time in the chair Davis bled from his nose and suffered burns to his head, legs and groin. Boy-oh-boy, did he suffer a lot of pain? Yes, he jolly well did.

It is claimed that execution by electrocution implies instantaneous death, but often this is not so. The pre-execution protocol is scary enough to wet anyone's pants and this is why an elastic band is applied to the penis, with male prisoners quite obviously, because it stops urine from shorting out the leg electrode. A tampon is inserted into the anus – for similar reasons. The head is also shaved. As for pain... of course there is pain. Two thousand three hundred volts are applied to the head to blast through the body. In some cases, several jolts have to be applied. In rare instances the prisoner might catch on fire with the unlucky recipient dearly wishing that he was someplace else – anywhere else for fuck's sake – as all that he was, or *will* ever be, goes up in a cloud of acrid smoke which fills the room with the stench of burning flesh.

What went wrong at Tiny's execution certainly ruffled a few legal feathers. In the Supreme Court of Florida, a four-day hearing began on 24 September 1999 to ascertain what had happened. The hearing found that the chair functioned as it should but that the breakers, components and circuitry were old. The chair must be programmed for the correct voltage and amperage levels to be set according to the levels of resistance that the inmate's body would have. This protocol had been followed. Davis hadn't died of asphyxiation caused by the mouth strap. The nosebleed began before the current was applied. And Davis suffered instantaneous death once the current was applied.

Of course, in this case, the electric chair did its job – it killed 'Tiny'. The blood from his nosebleed formed a cross like the 'Mark of God' on his chest. So, hands up those who believe that Davis deserves his own special place in Hell. Thank you. Thank *you* for your almost overwhelming support, but will the vegan couple at the back waving the banner, 'GOD FORGIVES ALL THOSE WHO SIN', *finally* realise that he doesn't, period, and I will now reliably tell you why because one Alfred P. Southwick (1826–1898) would not have been born, that's why.

Hailing from Buffalo, New York, a bright spark was our 'Al', for he started out as a steamboat engineer, then became a dentist and an inventor who suddenly had a hot epiphany upon hearing the story of an intoxicated man who touched a live electric generator. Ouch! Given that the guy had died/fried so quickly, Al instantly cooked up the notion that electricity could be used as an alternative to hanging for executions. Well, you would, wouldn't you, as anyone would if you knew that the mother-in-law had tripped over a live rail, say on the Portsmouth Harbour to Waterloo mainline, better still when it was raining.

Hanging works perfectly well when the drop is calculated to bring about instant death, so why change something that is *so* simple: using a length of rope and gravity? But, no! Al had a chat to one of his dental chair makers and after some tenuous experiments, suitably wearing rubber boots, he designed the first electric chair – an expensive, often unreliable contraption, that can turn the condemned into a burning human artefact straight out of Stephen King's novel-cum-movie *The Green Mile*, where Eduard Delacroix ends up resembling a Guy Fawkes on Bonfire Night.

★★★

Thomas Watt Hamilton

'We knew the guy. We went to his kids' club.
He had been in our car. We had driven and dropped
him off at a train station and things.'

Tennis champion, Andy Murray on
Thomas Watt Hamilton, the Dunblane School mass murderer –
the Sun, 26 November 2019

It would be extremely hard for me to leave out of this book the mass-shooters – teenagers and adults – who purposefully kill as many people as possible. This, unfortunately, often happens in schools especially in America – places where children should be as safe as if they were in their own homes. These killers are amongst the most disgusting individuals – cowards to a fault, so, for this chapter I have selected a special place in Hell for Thomas Watt Hamilton.

Although the study of serial homicide is my preferred discipline, I have interviewed a few mass murderers during my career, including the little weasel, Ronald 'Butch' DeFeo, of Amityville infamy. I have also carefully studied the warped psychopathology of Thomas Hamilton and

I want to try to take you right inside his head. It won't be a nice place to visit, I can assure you of this, but if we want to try and understand the twisted mindsets of such monsters, Hamilton will be a good starting point.

The 1996 Dunblane mass murder of sixteen school children and their teacher, plus the wounding of fifteen others, was a mass killing committed by one man, at a single location and in close proximity with no 'cooling off period between the shots fired'. It was a 'continuum' of trigger pulling – discharging bullets, often at pointblank range, into innocent, terrified little children.

I could spend the next three pages detailing the destructive power of any .357 Magnum firearm, but a picture, or in this case a video (available online by searching *Coonan 357 Magnum Semi-Auto pistol*), paints a million words. My publisher's lawyers will crucify me if I put into print precisely what I think about Jerry – the guy presenting this video – although the countable title 'dickhead' is stirring somewhere in my mind. Yet, for millions of US gun aficionados, this video, amongst thousands of other similar videos to be found online, can be termed as 'Ballistic Hard Porn'. It's compulsory, magazine-fuelled jerk-off material for anyone paying hefty subscription fees to the NRA. So, I truly beg you to watch this video... listen to every word macho Jerry says. Hey, if *you* take up his offer; even *you* could win all he wants to 'give away': including a JMA shotgun; a 'Vortex Razor' telescopic sight, *and* the must-have red-dot telescopic sighting system. So please watch our Jerry demonstrate the horrific power of a .357 Magnum 'down at the range' using *exactly* the identical calibre and probably almost the same cartridge load as used by Thomas Hamilton. But Hamilton was not firing at steel plate targets some distance away. He was using this weapon at pointblank range.

So, who *was* Thomas Watt Hamilton? Nick Cohen wrote in the *Independent* in 1996 that Hamilton 'had a deep-seated resentment burning for a quarter of a century, then something made him explode.' We know that Hamilton had a death wish. After the shooting he shot himself in the head. And, although this will seem highly unprofessional and even borderline crass – in dispatching himself he removed from the bereaved families the lengthy trauma and heartbreak of a trial then watching him spend the rest of his days in some cushy jail, or mental asylum. Fortunately, he ended his own life with one bullet paid for by him – a painless death to leave behind a monstrous legacy to the devastated parents and loved ones. This mental trauma will remain with them for the rest of their lives. Even tennis star Andy Murray still suffers from the Dunblane tragedy. He and his brother Jamie were inside the primary school when the attack took place and he has since opened up about his family connections to the man who carried it out.

Could the Dunblane School shootings have been prevented? The answer is yes *and* no. The 'no' is when a scenario arises where someone determined to commit mass-murder simply emerges out of nowhere as it can be difficult to steer them off their deadly course. Mass murderers are completely unpredictable. Most of these people appear to live *normal* lives. Although the majority are loners, perhaps holding down menial jobs, many have a deep sense of low self-esteem, are easily offended, prone to outbursts of anger at the drop of a hat and, more-or-less, socially disinclined – but otherwise they appear entirely harmless. Most of them have large chips on their shoulders; hold a deep-seated grudge of one kind or another, they might harbour a hatred for people of certain ages, religions, casts, colours and creeds. Others have no particular victimology: they simply go for a volume of deaths – killing anyone and everyone who comes into their sights.

The 'yes' part, however, is that the Dunblane shootings *could* have been prevented. For that matter, so could all of the recent and the yet-to-happen mass shootings in the US simply by banning the general public from purchasing such lethal firearms, lock, stock and barrel! But that's not the American way because that's what the US Constitution allows them to do. Here in the UK, had not Hamilton been able to possess his guns, whilst holding a licence issued by police, then all of those children and their teacher would still be alive today.

There is something eerily similar between mass-murderer Thomas Hamilton (1952–1996) and the serial killer, John Reginald Halliday Christie (1899–1953). I devoted a chapter to Christie in my book *Talking with Psychopaths and Savages: Beyond Evil*, published in 2019. There is, of course, the excellent fact that they are now both dead. Aside from that, their faces, thinning hair, high foreheads, almost identical spectacles and beady eyes are similar. In the aforementioned book I peeled away the fake mask that Christie wore to fool *everyone* who met him to expose to his eternal shame a cunningly devious, self-opinionated 'little man'. Christie was a control freak. He had 'waypoints' in his life where he changed direction to plunge further in his downward trajectory towards sado-sexual homicide most foul. Although Christie and Hamilton killed with different motives in mind – their targets and *modus operandi* also being totally different – they appear to me to have very similar psychopathologies. And this makes Hamilton even more chilling.

Oh, yes, indeed, it *is* chilling, almost wintery-day chilling when one starts to peel away the mask that Hamilton wore – the façade he presented to the outside world – to find a man with several personalities. Even more than just simply Dr Jekyll and Mr Hyde. Hamilton and Christie were two mentally decaying peas from the same pod. So, could this uncanny 'psychopathological resemblance' between these two killers hold some of the clues that make so many mass-murderers do what they do? The answer, I believe, is a resounding, yes!

'He was a lone madman in the Lee Harvey Oswald mould; an obsessive misfit who bottled up his paranoid resentment until he was ready to write himself into the national conscience with other peoples' blood.'
Journalist Nick Cohen on Hamilton

Nick Cohen is right when he says: 'Once he was dead, everyone knew how to sum up Thomas Hamilton.' It tells us everything. It tells us that despite many, perhaps well-founded, suspicions one has about someone's seemingly unhealthy behaviour, many refuse to believe, or *could not* believe, that such an insignificant little man as Hamilton can metamorphose into a monster. There can be no doubt that one of these monsters *could* be moving amongst us right now, and one could be living next door to you! We can also reflect upon the words of US serial killer, Ted Bundy: 'Society wants to believe it can identify evil people, or bad or harmful people, but it's not practical. There are no stereotypes. We serial killers are your sons, we are your husbands, we are everywhere, and there will be more of your children dead tomorrow.' Yep, Ted, you nailed that in one!

As the grim annals of crime tragically show, everyone *thinks* they know the man before he commits his terrible crimes, but they do not *really know* him until it's too late. Think of it this way: we might see a neat looking home in some quite urban cul-de-sac. Its front garden carefully groomed. It looks peaceful and lovely. But it's all a front because dread secrets may lie within. Time and again, over decades, police find torture chambers, and corpses rotting under floorboards or in some dark, dank cellar. We can use this analogy to describe the mask or the 'outer person' – we cannot always see the monster behind the pleasant façade.

The mask of normalcy these serial killers, spree killers or mass-murderers wear is their social camouflage and it enables them to mix easily within society. Indeed, even when cracks sometimes appear in their masks and suspicions *are* raised these psychopaths apply some makeup and the cracks disappear. It is back to the doffing of a cap, a good turn for an elderly neighbour, who later tells everyone, 'But he is such a nice man. Always so considerate, too.' The rumours slowly cease, life returns to normal... well *almost* normal, it would be fair to say. Oh, gosh, didn't all of Dr. Harold Shipman's patients say that he was the nicest doctor one could have?

At the time of the shootings, Hamilton lived in Kent Road, Stirling. Neighbours who caught a glance through his window would have seen disturbing pictures of semi-naked boys in swimming trunks covering his walls. What might that tell you and me if *we* were being nosy? Of course, I am not suggesting for a millisecond that any of my readers have a habit of peering through a neighbour's windows – nor do I, come to that! I mean all of my readers are truly wonderful, decent folk, are you not? But let's say, as an academic exercise, one happened to look through a neighbour's window and glimpsed the rather odd artwork that Mr Hamilton obviously enjoyed. Enjoyed so much that he didn't care two hoots if any passerby spotted his taste in soft porn, either.

At this point, I guarantee the reader that a number of psychiatrists, psychologists and cops will come down on me like a ton of bricks. They would insist on disagreeing entirely. 'Hey, Mr Berry-Dee, there is nothing illegal in that.' As I said at the outset of this book, I stress that I always say it as it is, so as we start looking behind Hamilton's mask of normalcy and peering through his front window, I not only see soft porn, I see a householder who has what one might term an 'unhealthy interest in young boys'. The fact that it is on such brazen display is also a sign that, consciously, the man is also sticking two fingers up to his neighbours because deep down he doesn't give a fuck what his neighbours think of him. This man is self-centered, inconsiderate, arrogant to a fault, and a complete loser when it comes down to any form of successful relationship with one of the opposite sex – maybe even his own gender perhaps. My lady readers might like to look up Hamilton's photo on the internet... not exactly the catch of *any* century, you might agree?

Cathleen Kerr was a neighbour of Hamilton and, according to Nick Cohen, she appears to have been the nearest person he had as a *friend* in the entire neighbourhood – and it's a *big* neighbourhood, I can tell you this much. Cathy recalled that Hamilton sometimes called round to her place for coffee. Importantly, he never reciprocated and invited the old dear to *his* front room. Can you imagine the result? Cathy's blue rinse would have instantly turned white, her cheeks flushed Darcey Rose red, as he proudly pointed out his numerous pictures of nubile young boys in wet swimming trunks. Hamilton was known by the local school kids as 'Mr Creepy'. With his podgy face, his insinuating voice and his 'Dr. Crippen-style' spectacles, he made their flesh crawl. For all their bonding over cups of tea, Mrs Kerr only really got to know the truth about her friend, Hamilton, *after* he'd committed mass murder. Reflecting on Hamilton, Cathy said, 'He always made kind enquiries about the health of my sick husband, Peter. He was quietly spoken, well dressed and placed. Yes, he wore an anorak, but he *always* wore a collar and tie underneath.' Oh bless. Not exactly the height of sartorial elegance, is it? Hamilton did have an air of normalcy and respectability as he wandered, head down, hands shoved deep into his pockets, his persuasive manner and easily deployed unctuous charm oozing from him. Actually, I see him standing on a plinth in 'The Chamber of Horrors' at Madam Tussauds, right next to John Reginald Christie – two murderous individuals, who in real life, so perfectly multi-masked, that although seeming a bit odd at times one would not have noticed that they existed at all.

By now you, the reader, will be starting to see Hamilton as he *really was*. It is not exactly social rocket science to begin to figure him out, is it? By putting up his soft porn for any passerby to view, Hamilton was allowing *us* to take a look into *his own* twisted morality. It was as if he were consciously inviting the world to take a glimpse into his warped psychopathology. I do not think one needs a degree in forensic psychology or psychiatry, to figure this out either.

Various media articles describe the start of Hamilton's 'problems' as manifesting at the age of twenty-two. His major grievance, one that festered inside him for the remainder of his life, was that he was chucked out of the 4th and 6th Stirling District Scouts on the grounds that, 'he was not suitable to be a troop leader.' Several complaints had been made about him including the fact that he had forced boys to sleep with him in his van on hill-walking expeditions.

However, in furtherance of some media articles, it is said that Hamilton became convinced that people were seeing him as a pervert, so perhaps the Akela who effectively fired Hamilton junior had good reason to do so for there is always smoke around a Scouts' camp fire. Putting this another way: the Scoutmaster, in his wise judgement – with his pack's overall welfare at heart – knew that Hamilton was not a healthy influence on his other charges. Whether it was thoughtlessness, or that he was in a complete muddle, Hamilton was patently a rotten apple in a basket of many other perfectly happy and considerate youngsters. He was a bad influence, so he had to go!

For reasons only known to him, Hamilton fought a running battle with officialdom for the next twenty-one years. To put this succinctly, he became a pain-in-the-ass; an obsequious social misfit who easily manipulated and saw off all the police and bureaucrats he came into conflict with. We have all met one of these obnoxious 'little men' at some time or another – always moaning and utter damned nuisances. Now think: 'Antisocial'; 'narcissistic personality'; 'borderline sociopath'; 'a controlling man', and perhaps you can now see a little further into Hamilton's mind. Years previously, the Scout Association had raised a red flag, now there were even more going up all around.

Four Scottish police forces had investigated Hamilton following complaints and accusations made by at least twelve parents of young boys. Each time detectives failed to find enough solid evidence that would stand up in court, but the social services were onto him. In the early eighties, Central Regional Council made a gallant effort to close down his boys' club meetings in Dunblane High School, but he was a litigious man and outwitted them, forcing the authorities to back down.

The duplicitous Hamilton was not only lucky when he escaped prosecution, he wrote letters of complaint, even to the Queen. He was manipulative enough to garner support from the local government ombudsman for Scotland, gun club managers, gun shop owners, even the police officers who had approved his firearm certificates. Councillors and many parents also came to his aid – some from Stirling, Dunblane and other towns and cities where he ran other boys' clubs. They believed that he was the victim of unsubstantiated gossip. Others thought differently.

'I saw him in the street about once a month for ten years and he was always complaining. I never got the impression that he was concealing misconduct. He did have an ingratiating, almost oily manner, but I put that down to the buffetings he received.'

Retired councillor, Francis Saunders on Hamilton

Hamilton was obsessed with real or *imagined* enemies, but those who say he was not frightened of his adversaries are over-simplifying. He was certainly obsessed, but I would add that he was becoming more paranoid as each week passed him by. He was losing control. One might assume in a similar situation one would ignore any truly false accusations – not make a song and dance about the issues and get on with their lives letting the tittle-tattle fade away, but not Hamilton. He must have had a guilty conscience that preyed upon him. This overt 'support seeking' mechanism was to paper over the cracks in the fake mask he presented to everyone, but also an effort to paint over his oversized, self-opinionated ego – one that was slowly starting to deflate.

I can also see that one part of his mental processing system was telling him that everyone was conspiring and out to get him. To compensate, the other half of his mind was saying that he was innocent of any wrongdoing. It would be only a matter of time before one side or the other would win. Then all of his fuses would blow.

Of course Hamilton was frightened. He'd experienced the police knocking on his door before and had gotten away with anything he *might have done* through lack of evidence, but people like Hamilton always live in fear of a parental complaint – one that finally does stick! I dare say that every time he saw a police car pull up near his house his blood pressure went through the roof. Ask any criminal who has committed a crime and thought they were home free whether they have felt that same panic. To see a Bobby beneath a tall hat walking one's way will be the most effective laxative they will ever have.

In Hamilton we find an extreme narcissist. These sorts are bullies, control freaks and they will use anyone or any organisation to favour them, support them or comfort them – all of which re-establishes faith in their crumbling egos. Actually, we saw this echoed in President Donald Trump as he blundered towards political extinction. Take away this support mechanism and the ego is damaged. Finally, the person has to face up to reality; to face themselves in the mirror, physical and psychological warts and all. And he, or she, will not be one teeny weeny bit happy about that. Anyone who has been in an abusive relationship with overbearing, spiteful, bullying, controlling, narcissistic male partners, will understand what I am referring to here. Once the other partner rebels, reveals their inner strength and leaves, the abuser has lost control and is quick to write contrite love letters, make promises that they will never keep. They might pester the other on the phone, ever so desperate to win them back. In a nutshell, narcissists are weak to their *very* core!

As the psychoanalyst, Dr. Alice Miller, puts it beautifully, and I paraphrase: 'The fragile ego is like a balloon floating high on very thin string. There is a final puff of wind, the string suddenly snaps and the ego bursts, without warning sometimes, with devastating outcomes.' For my part, I have identified the moment of this 'ego popping' numerous times in the histories of many of the serial killers I have interviewed over the years. Most of them have very fragile egos, indeed. We can even see this with the British serial killer, Dr. Harold Shipman. Once he had been locked up for life, his ego and self-esteem collapsed. Stripped of all the adulation he had received as being a most loved GP, he was forced to face what he truly was. Now, he was a mere prison number in a system jam-packed with the type of people he despised, being ordered to do this and that by upstart prison officers whom he disliked in equal measure. He lost control. He was ruined, so he hung himself inside his prison cell. I am reliably informed by a source whom I cannot name, Shipman is in Hell right now too.

'The grandiose person is never really free. First because he is so excessively dependent on admiration from others; and second, because his self-respect is dependent on qualities, functions and achievements that can suddenly fail.'
Dr. Alice Miller, The Drama of Being a Child

Narcissistic Hamilton had a suppressed anger management problem exacerbated by a guilt complex that metamorphosed into a paranoid state of mind which housed a fragile ego and low self-esteem. Subconsciously he knew he was a drowning man and all of his attempts to garner assistance to keep him afloat were to no avail. This self-esteem and faux grandiosity – his entire psychological infrastructure – was crumbling away like weathered cement. Sooner or later he had to explode when the control over his rage he once had in place finally deserted him. It would take just one more adverse influence to knock his house down. The really *big* problem was that this human time bomb owned lethal firearms and he knew how to use them. No guns would have meant no Dunblane Primary School mass murder, end of story.

***

Jeffrey Lionel Dahmer

No second-guessing where Jeff is right now. One of his childhood friends predicted his fate years ago. Jim Klippel described finding a dog's head impaled on a stake near Dahmer's home. Jim told police many years later that he also found 'a fire pit ringed by thirteen smaller ones'. 'It looked like an occult sacrifice area. It looked like some form of Devil worshipping to us,' Jim told police. Bridget Geiger, who as a young girl was invited to a party at the teenage Dahmer's said, 'There was a séance, and one of Dahmer's pals said something about contacting Lucifer.' When the lights dimmed and the candle sputtered, Bridget very wisely left. Wouldn't you, too? Maybe muttering under your breath, 'FUCKKKK THAT!' Dahmer's crimes are much more than a passing interest in black magic or devil worship though.

Tracy Edwards, the man who almost became Dahmer's eighteenth victim, said that Jeffrey's face changed and that he felt as if he 'was confronting Satan himself.' A few of the serial killers I have interviewed over the years have exhibited this sudden change from apparent normality into pure evil personified right in front of my very eyes, up close and personal. Whilst interviewing the unshackled Arthur John Shawcross aka 'The Monster of the Rivers', I noticed that he had started to sweat. Then his face turned a plaster-cast white and went as tight as a bat's skin. His ever-blinking eyes turned coal black. His features contorted. His teeth clenched tight. It was as if there was a demon fighting to get out and explode into the room. It was fascinating to observe at such close quarters. I know that you will think that I am going all Stephen King here, but if you've not experienced one of these encounters the only way I can describe it is to say that many of these monsters often appear *possessed* by something not human.

I have no doubt that Satan's spawn does exist, and *maybe* it lived inside Jeffrey Dahmer. Many have claimed to have a connection to the Devil. Richard Ramirez aka 'The Night Stalker' of Los Angeles would leave Satanic symbols at the scene of his terrible murders. There are many who believe that Charles Manson was 'possessed' and he claimed to be the Messiah to his followers. But Manson was just a weedy little con artist at heart despite all the ill-deserved adoration he has hoovered up over the decades to bathe in like a mucky duck in a puddle of water. The same applies to Ronald 'Butch' DeFeo, the Amityville mass murderer, whom I have interviewed in prison. Countless horror movies and books have been written about his so-called possession by Satan, but it's all BS.

So, are these types possessed by 'earth-bound spirits'? The well-meaning Swedish–American psychiatrist, Dr. Carl August Wickland and his wife Anna, believed that these 'spirits' could possess the body of a living person, and cause him or her to commit violent crimes.

Wickland's last post was as chief psychiatrist at the State Psychopathic Institute of Chicago. Then, he turned away from conventional medical psychology and toward the belief that psychiatric illnesses were the result of influence by spirits of the dead. The bespectacled Wickland came to believe – bless him – that a large number of his patients had become possessed by what he called 'obsessing spirits'. He would use 'low-voltage electric shocks' to dislodge them, while his wife acted as a medium to guide them to 'the spirit world'. Indeed, spiritualists considered him an authority on 'destructive spirits'. His book *Thirty Years Among the Dead*, published in 1924, details his experiences as a psychical researcher. He was convinced that he was in contact with a group of spirits known as the 'Mercy Band' who would remove the possessors, and help them in the spirit world. Can you imagine how some of his wide-eyed mentally unhinged patients would have felt when in strolls the good doctor Wickland and his wife Anna to strap them down, attach electrodes to their heads for a dose of the good old 'low-voltage'? There is Anna, sitting in a chair, summoning forth the 'Mercy Band', one hand on a Bible, the other aloft. Well, I will tell you this much, if those poor souls had *any* chance of becoming compos mentis ever again, that would have shot any odds in their favour right out of the barred fucking window, so back to Dahmer.

'It's a process, it doesn't happen overnight when you depersonalise another person and view them as just an object. An object for pleasure and not a living breathing human being. It seems to make it easier to do things you shouldn't do.'

Jeffrey Dahmer

Jeffrey Dahmer is known for luring impressionable young lads to his home where he would drug them, before killing them. He would sleep with the corpses and keep them in his home for many days. Then he would dismember them before preserving parts or even cannabilising them. Dahmer killed seventeen young men between 1978 and 1991.

Jeffrey Dahmer was born on 21 May 1960. His life ended when he was beaten to death by a prison inmate Christopher Scarver on 28 November 1994, at the Columbia Correctional Institution, Portage, Wisconsin, USA. His body was cremated, and his ashes given to family or friends, whom one might hope sent them off in a hand basket straight to Hell.

As cunning as a fox, Dahmer hunted in the gay community and was careful to select young males on the fringes of society. His victims were often itinerant or involved in illegal activity. Their disappearances were not significant and this reduced the likelihood of his capture. Much like Friedrich 'Fritz' Haarmann, Dahmer lured them to his home with promises of money or sex. We also see echoes of bisexual John Wayne Gacy here, although he targetted young men any place he could find them, sometimes at bus terminals or hanging around outside gay bars.

'Morbid fascination is a disobedience against reason.'

Plutarch

There are several aspects of Dahmer's psychopathology worth exploring. An unnamed police officer said in 1991 that he believed Dahmer was motivated by an intense loneliness that dated back to his childhood and his parents' divorce: 'He didn't want anyone else to leave him,' various sources state. For the most part though, Dahmer gave his 'guests' no time to make the choice to stay with him or indeed to make for the door and escape. They were drugged soon after they arrived, then strangled. On the face of it, this suggests that the real motive was not loneliness but instead a morbid obsession with mutilation. Brian Masters, the biographer of the British serial killer Dennis Nilsen, advanced the same explanation for Nilsen's fifteen murders in his fantastic book *Killing for Company*. However, in the case of Dahmer, this is an unlikely explanation of his crimes.

One doesn't just start killing and cutting up human beings. There will be an escalation of behaviour and there is usually something in a person's past that triggers 'reward' feelings in that person's mind. Dahmer's malignant passion may have started when he was a child with what he called his 'bug collection'. He would collect butterflies, moths, dragonflies, mantises, spiders and beetles and preserve them in formaldehyde. As Dahmer grew older and bigger he moved onto larger creatures – birds and rats. Could it be suggested that maybe this made Dahmer feel like a doctor – a pathologist even. Perhaps stripping animals into skeletons provided an outlet for his aggression and satisfied a need for self-assertion. So, if we were inside Jeffrey's head around that time, we might find a young boy alone in his own morbid world bubble with his thoughts and growing fantasies. He would have been withdrawing into a world of dark ideas. Once these bleak fantasies form in a young mind without intervention they are locked in for evermore. This morbidity festered to culminate in his first homicide.

On 18 June 1978, Dahmer, now eighteen, had been left alone in his parents' home in Bath Township. He decided to go out to seek some company. His parents were going through a divorce and his father, Lionel, had moved into a nearby motel. His mother, Joyce, was relocating to Chippewa Falls with his young brother, David.

Dahmer encountered nineteen-year-old Stephen Hicks who was hitchhiking to a rock concert. He lured the lad to the house on the pretext of the two of them drinking alcohol. According to Dahmer, after a few hours drinking and listening to music Hicks wanted to leave 'and [I] didn't want him to,' Dahmer later told police. It was then that he bludgeoned Hicks with a 10lb dumbbell twice over the back of the head while Hicks sat upon a chair. When his victim fell to the ground unconscious, Dahmer throttled him to death with the bar of the dumbbell, stripped off the lad's clothes before masturbating over the corpse. The following day, Hicks was dissected in the basement and his remains were buried in a shallow grave in the backyard. Several weeks later, Dahmer dug it all up, pared the flesh off of the bones and dissolved the flesh in acid before flushing the solution down a toilet. Using a sledgehammer, he crushed the bones and scattered them in the woods behind the house.

The murder of Stephen Hicks must have had a crystalising effect on Dahmer's sexual inclinations. He was no longer a misunderstood loner; he was a killer, an outcast from society. Dahmer, like Nilsen, began drinking heavily in his teens. Alcohol combined with struggles to deal with his homosexuality, insecurity, lack of self-esteem and a morbid obsession with death, led, perhaps inevitably, to necrophilia. The classic study of necrophilia is contained in LAPD psychiatrist Dr J Paul de River's highly recommended and highly praised *The Sexual Criminal: A Psychoanalytical Study*, in which he cites the case of a twenty-three-year-old mortuary attendant who, from his late teens, had violated at least five female corpses *a week*!

The psychopathology of necrophiles is fascinating if one is into this subject and probably worth an entire book on its own – but I think it all comes down to 'control' and 'sexual perversion in extremis'. Dahmer, Nilsen, Gacy, and countless more sexual psychos kept the bodies of the dead close to them. In fact Gacy is extraordinary in that he buried most of his victims in the crawl space under his own home in Des Plaines, Chicago. But why, you might ask; after all is said and done he was a home builder, he had a pickup which he could have used to dump corpses well away from the place where he lived. Although, it is correct to say that from time-to-time he disposed of the bodies out in the wilds – the Des Plaines River being one location for instance.

Perhaps the root of Jeffrey's perverse morbidity can be found in his early dissection of insects and small animals. We must remember that he lived in his own lonely bubble world. His parents were separating. It is from such situations as this that a young child can start to disassociate from reality. In Kenneth Bianchi we find a similar split mindset; one where as a very young lad he had an imaginary friend called 'Stevie' with whom he played and talked. Indeed, when his mother caught Kenneth doing something wrong he would tell her that it was all 'Stevie's' fault. Many people with schizotypal personality disorders have difficulties forming relationships and experience extreme anxiety in social situations. They may react inappropriately or not react at all during a conversation or they may talk to themselves. They tend to be rigid, inflexible, and unable to respond to the changes and demands of life. This may lead to Borderline Personality Disorder (BDP), which can affect up to 5 percent of of the US population. All of this seems to fit Dahmer hand in glove.

Necrophilia is defined in *The Diagnostic and Statistical Manual of Mental Disorders* as a 'specified paraphilic disorder involving recurrent and intense sexual interest in corpses.' Perhaps the most exhaustive and useful of all the varied classifications has come from Anil Aggrawal, a professor of forensic medicine at the Maulana Azad Medical College, New Delhi. In 2009, he proposed ten different types of necrophile, ranging from those who get pleasure, but not necessarily sexual, from being near the dead, to those who are aroused by touching the dead, to those who exclusively require sexual contact with the dead. Homicidal necrophiles such as Jeffrey Dahmer and Denis Nilsen are capable of having intercourse with the living, but are willing to kill to satisfy their need for sex with a corpse. So, if we boil this down (s'cuse the grim pun), Dahmer's prime motives are: the obtaining of plunder or other coveted objects (his victims) and the gratification of some selfish or malignant passion (extreme, homicidal necrophiliac morbid possession).

After Dahmer's eventual arrest, in the early hours of Tuesday, 23 July 1991, forensic investigators from the medical examiner's office began making a list of all the human remains in the killer's small apartment. Their inventory included: hands; heads; pieces of muscle; genitals and various internal organs. In addition, there were painted skulls and other bones. It was a slaughterhouse cum torture chamber. The freezer compartment of the fridge contained meat in a plastic bag which looked very much like a human heart. Another freezer contained three plastic bags, each one with a severed head inside. A filing cabinet contained three skulls; a box contained two more skulls and an album full of gruesome photographs. Two more skulls were found in a pan. There were eleven heads and skulls in all. Another pan contained some severed hands and a male penis. A stinking blue plastic barrel contained three male torsos. An electric saw stained with blood made it clear how Dahmer had dismembered his victims. There was also a large vat of murky hydrochloric acid.

In finalising this chapter, let's once again return to our amiable Dr Wickland and his good wife Anna. Criminologists, by their very picky nature, naturally dismiss beliefs such as being possessed by the Devil or demons, as delusions, whimsical at best. Around the turn of the century Dr. Carl Wickland – and we have no idea as to what medication he must have been under – was driven to take the belief of demonic possession seriously when he married Anna. She claimed to be a medium, and like all 'mediums' she went into trances and heard 'voices' that she claimed came from the dead who spoke through her lips. Methodical to a fault, Dr. Wickland often checked up to find out if these 'spirits' were the people they claimed to be and found out that they frequently seemed to be genuine. Can you smell a rat here? I can!

In July 1906, Mrs Wickland began speaking in a man's voice who identified himself (without producing his ID) as an architect and socialite named Stanford White. You will be relieved to learn that, at no expense to the reader, I have done quite a bit of research into Stanford. He had been shot dead three weeks beforehand at precisely 10.15 p.m., Monday, 25 June, by a wealthy young scoundrel called Harry K. Thaw, whose wife, Evelyn Nesbit, had been seduced by White many years earlier.

'I was not crazy when I shot Stanford White. I'm glad I did it.'
Harry K. Thaw

The shooting took place in the open-air theatre at New York's Madison Square Garden roof theatre, in the heart of Manhattan. The place was packed that warm night. Men wore lightweight suits and straw boaters while the ladies wore evening dresses and cool hats. The tables were set among arched vines strung with coloured lights, and potted palm trees swayed in the breeze from the Hudson river. The show was expected to be a hit and drew most of New York's elite. They arrived in twos and threes in chauffeured limousines from nearby restaurants. This was the opening night of *Mam'zelle Champagne* – a musical revue from the book by Edgar Allan Woolf.

Now comes the juicy stuff.

Evelyn, the heroine, at the centre of this love triangle was, by any account, drop-dead, traffic stoppingly beautiful, but she wore two faces: an innocent girl-child and a hard, little chorus girl. She was a model, had had a number of men, and had dabbled in sculpture. The most famous photo of her was taken in Stanford White's studio when she was aged sixteen. Dubbed by the media 'The Tigress', she later described the photo session in court where she presented the very tall, sandy-haired White, as a perverse lecher. The case of Harry Thaw is well worth a read with a lot of vice *v.* virtue, bullying, plotting, Bible-thumping, deceit and incrimination with champagne and flowers thrown in with bullwhips for good measure. It was most convenient that Anna Wickland should suddenly pick up on the victim of a scandal-drenched shooting that had rocked 'The Big Apple'. Out came the Ouija board and Tarot cards and up popped Stanford. After Stanford had his say, along came a voice claiming that he was Thaw's long-deceased father. Thaw Sr. declared that his son had been possessed by a 'spirit' when he murdered Mr. White. He offered some 'convincing evidence' that he was who he claimed to be. He gave the correct name of his son's attorney – a name that had been in the world's press for several weeks. I mean one could not make this up if one tried. Nevertheless, experiences like this convinced Dr. Wickland that 'spirit possession' often occurs, and he cites many so-called remarkable cases in his book. Enough already? Not quite because one must remember that this Wickland chappie was a shrink. And we all know that shrinks can be as off-the-wall as the people they treat.

According to Wickland, the 'spirits' are not demons or devils, but simply spirits of people who have died and who do not realise they are dead – 'earth-bound spirits'.

He was firmly convinced that such spirits can enter the bodies of people who are mentally deficient, as well as people who are, 'on the same wavelength'. A bit like our WiFi today, when it works, that is! So, according to this quack, the spirit of a criminal might 'possess' someone who is subject to violent rages or is prone to resentment and jealousy, and cause that person to commit crimes. He believed that the people suffering from violent and negative feelings actually attract such 'spirits'.

I am a fair man, and most people would dismiss such a view as pure superstition. But there can be no doubt that there are many cases of 'Dr. Jekyll and Mr Hyde' criminals that sound remarkably like Wickland's cases of possession. Psychiatrists often try to explain such cases in terms of 'split personality'. One of the most remarkable of recent examples was an Ohio rapist called Billy Milligan who claimed to possess twenty-two other personalities, one of which was a lesbian who was responsible for the rapes. Like most cases of people with 'multiple personalities', Milligan had been sexually abused during childhood.

Fredrich Nietzsche was giving us *all* a warning when he said: 'He who fights monsters might take care lest he thereby becomes a monster. And if you gaze for too long into the abyss, the abyss gazes also into you.' We have seen so little of Dahmer's emerging psychopathology in this book simply because my restricted word count doesn't permit it. We are all subject to our weaknesses and strengths. There are those who are hard-wired conspiracists and those who dismiss conspiracists as cranks. But often the truth is a mix of both. It is the art of sorting the wheat from the chaff – you pay your money and you take your choice – you are either hotwired to believe that evil spirits can control a personality, or you may choose to dismiss the very thought. But, there, you may want to sit on the fence to await the answer. Whatever the case, we can be sure that Jeffrey was possessed by something – the overwhelming need to kill, dismember, skin, chop up, boil and eat young boys. He did have a satanic shrine in his seedy apartment, but whether he talked at length with Old Nick or not we will never know.

We might have believed all that Dr. Wickland told us if it had not been for the presence of his medium wife whose tainted 'profession' has been debunked so many times as spiritual fraud. It almost seems that she came to possess him with her wild and woolly ideas, because he adored her. So there seems to be some marital manipulation at work here, after all they do say that the easiest person to sell something to is another salesman. Those who dabble in Ouija boards and the occult are maybe seeking comfort from the alleged 'voices' of their dear departed. But if one is a lonely, disenfranchised kid such as Jeffrey Dahmer living in his own fantasy world of murder most foul – he is opening up the door to *true evil* in whatever form it takes. Whether he was possessed by Satan or not is a question for another day. But Jeffrey looked into the abyss as a youngster and then he fell in. Best we leave it at that!

★★★

Reverend James 'Jim' Warren Jones

When we consider profound immorality and wickedness many names spring to mind. There is the handsome devil, Eugen Weidmann. Carl Panzram and Werner Boost whose bitter hatred of mankind led them to kill again and again. Sex killers John Norman Collins and Leonard Lake. Graham Young, the teenager whose interest in poison became a game of death. Killing machines, Paul John Knowles and Harvey 'Harvey The Hammer' Carignan – two serial murderers who cruised America's highways looking for victims as did interstate trucker Keith Hunter Jesperson aka 'The Happy Face Killer'. Richard Ramirez aka 'The Night Stalker'; Peter Manuel, the Glasgow braggart who became Scotland's most notorious murderer – all of them came from the loins of Satan, as did George Joseph Smith 'The Brides in the Bath' serial killer. Eric Edgar Cooke, a cat burglar whose random killings held Perth in a grip of terror. Dr. Marcel Petiot, the mass killer who claimed that his innocent victims were wartime traitors. Albert DeSalvo aka 'The Boston Strangler', John Reginald Christie, Kenneth Erskine and 'Bible

John', two killers who like Thierry Paulin exploited the cover of city life to prey on their helpless victims. There is Lonnie Franklin Jr. aka 'The Grim Sleeper', mass shooter Charles Whitman, Edward Gein the Midwest psychopath who turned his farmhouse into a human abattoir like David Alan Gore, the US serial killer cum Deputy Sheriff who confessed to, and was convicted of, six murders in Vero Beach and Indian River County, Florida. The list is endless of those who deserve a very special place in Hell. However, one transcends them all:

Reverend Jim Jones aka 'The High Priest of Death' – he called himself their 'Dad'. A Bible-thumping, self-professed faith healer and preacher, Jim Jones, abused and corrupted the 'children' in his flock who had followed him from their American homes to the slums of Guyana. This cult leader brainwashed them, using devious methods of mind-control. He was the salesman of death, and hundreds of men, women and little children were tricked into making the final sacrifice for him, for on 18 November 1978, hundreds of worshippers at the 'Peoples Temple' in Jonestown, many of them children, died after drinking Kool-Aid laced with cyanide upon the orders of their leader, the Reverend Jim Jones.

Within minutes, ingestion of cyanide will cause dizziness, a headache, nausea and vomiting. This is followed by rapid breathing, a rapid heart rate, weakness, convulsions, loss of consciousness, low blood pressure, lung damage and respiratory failure which leads to cardiac arrest. Few people who suffer cyanide poisoning die painlessly. Indeed, if you want to wish that you'd never been born then cyanide is the way to go. So, who was Jim Jones?

Born 13 May 1931, Jones was of Irish/Welsh descent. He was raised in the small town of Lynn, Randolph County, Indiana known as 'The Hoosier State'. Sadly, he is Lynn's only 'Notable Person'. The Jones family lived in a shack without plumbing. His father, James Thurman, had been gassed in France during World War One. His mother was Lynetta Putnam. Jones later claimed partial Cherokee ancestry through his mother who had never seen a teepee in her life.

After the war, James Thurman returned to Lynn to become the local barfly; a habitual drunkard, as mean as a rattlesnake and redneck racist – he was also a lifelong member of the Ku Klux Klan. Lynetta was off-the-wall by any stretch of the imagination. She shocked her Indiana small town by wearing trousers and smoking in the street – a cardinal sin back then. She fancied that she'd travelled the world in a previous existence, subscribed to *National Geographic* and filled her son's bedtime stories with tales of her adventures, headhunters on the Amazon river, spells, omens, the transmigration of souls and black magic. Now that's what I call a *real* mum. All I had was some bullshit Beatrix Potter stuff about some rabbits. Give me some headhunters and black magic anytime. Despite this, Lynetta did have a puritanical streak in her. She told her son that dreams were a vision of the future and that he was destined to help the poor and the weak.

Although Jim Jones does not seem to have caught religion from his family, being raised in the Midwest 'Bible-Belt' he could not help feel its influence – along with stern fundamentalism and lashings of white supremacy. At the age of twelve, in a loft surrounded by pictures of the Crucifixion and lynchings, he began preaching his hellfire and damnation sermons. Around the age of twelve I was making Airfix airplane models and hanging them from my bedroom ceiling with cotton thread. The only picture I had was of 'Peter the Rabbit' at which I threw darts. Nevertheless, young Jones rapidly earned a reputation as a healer of ailing pets, and held mock funeral services for dead cats – the latter being the ones he didn't heal. Others, those with their redneck wits about them, saw a more sinister side to him. 'Some of the neighbours would have cats missing and we always thought he was using them for sacrifices,' recalled one of Jones' contemporaries.

While most of his school friends went into the privileged and mainly white world of banking, business, farming or teaching, Jones worked as a porter in a hospital near Indianapolis where his colleagues were mainly poor and black. Here, aged sixteen, he met and married a skinny student nurse called Marceline who was five years his senior. They would go on to build a family of nine children. Jones wanted to become a doctor and he enrolled at the University of Indiana in Bloomington. A year later he dropped out, having become intent on becoming a preacher. He kicked off his new 'calling' by recruiting door-to-door for a Methodist Mission, in due course gaining valuable experience as an unordained supply preacher.

'The most compassionate, honest and courageous
human being on earth.'
Tim Stoen's description of Jim Jones
in an affidavit of 1972

To follow Jones' religious narrative is an exhausting exercise, one even harder to follow if one is not familiar with 'The Good Book', but here goes.

Jones was not what one might label the prototype tele-evangelist who preached God, the Flag and the American Way. In 1953, he joined the Communist Party. That year, he also conceived the idea of 'revolutionary death' when the atom spies Julius and Ethel Rosenberg were executed by the federal government of the USA in Sing Sings' electric chair. Their deaths, he concluded, shattered the illusion that America was the 'last, best hope of mankind.'

According to the 'Wings of Deliverance Corporate Papers', in 1956, the un-ordained Jones established a church called the 'Peoples Temple of the Disciples of Christ' – all a bit of a mouthful for it was soon shortened to the 'Peoples Temple' which shortly thereafter became the 'Wings of Deliverance', which he supported by selling monkeys – as you do. Located in a church building which he purchased at 15th and North New Jersey Streets, a racially mixed area in Indianapolis, and using a blend of idealism and manipulation, the soon to be Reverend Jim Jones manoeuvred himself into a position of power and prestige. The trustees of this 'corporation' were: Rev. James W. Jones and Marcelina Jones of 3058 Villa Avenue, Indianapolis, and one Lynette P. Jones of 1130 E. Main Street. He would soon become a highly controversial figure, but with power would soon come paranoia.

Jones' message was one that combined elements of Christianity with communist and socialist ideology, with an emphasis on racial equality, he was an 'integrationalist'. Privately, however, he described himself as a 'socialist' – though his political philosophy seems to owe more to Robin Hood than to Karl Marx. The poorer and weaker his followers, the more attention he lavished upon them with the whites being too tight to fund him, while the poorer black folk he found easier to exploit. One early member recalled, 'He had a lot of them, the kind of people who most folks don't want to have anything to do with. Fat, ugly old ladies who didn't have nobody in the world. He'd pass around hugs and kisses like he really loved them, and you could see on their faces what he meant to them.'

So, can you see this handsome, oily, slick Bible-thumper, this false prophet who met God on a train – for fuck's sake – working his audience now? Picture him wearing his sunglasses, white jacket and dog collar, his right arm held stiffly aloft, fist clenched in a Nazi-style of salute. Yes, that *is* the 'Stars and Stripes' hanging limply behind him, too. There is a bigoted arrogance about him, a sort of Mussolini cum Donald Trump with jaw-jutting arrogance. He was a snake-oil salesman, preaching love to the black folk whom his own father despised. His success at building a truly multi-racial congregation – one of the first in America – attracted unwelcome attention. Segregationalists hated him and threw dead cats into his church. His windows were broken and explosives were detonated in his yard. The more opposition he faced, the harder he tried. He and his wife adopted several non-white children to join their biological son, Stephan Gandhi. His stand against racism would later lead to his appointment of the newly created City Human Rights Commission, reporting directly to Mayor Christian J. Emhardt in 1991.

By 1957, Jones had collected a whopping $50,000 and set himself up in a lavishly converted synagogue on North Delaware Street, Indianapolis. This was the first Peoples Temple Full Gospel Church. Outside was a grubby, illuminated sign – of the sort one would see over a West End strip joint – bearing the legend:

> Peoples Temple of the Disciples of Christ
> Denominational Brotherhood.
> Jim Jones – Pastor. Fri. 8 P.M.
> Sun. 11 A.M. – 7 P.M.

Around the same time, Pastor Jones made several pilgrimages to the Peace Mission of Father Divine; the most successful ministry to the urban poor in the county. There, he would learn at the master's feet.

Father Divine (1876–1965) is an interesting character indeed. He was an African American spiritual leader from about 1907 until his death. Like all of his ilk, ego-inflation was a priority so he gave himself a grander name: 'Reverend Major Jealous Divine'. He was also known as 'The Messenger' earlier in his life. He founded the International Peace Mission Movement, formulated its doctrine, and oversaw its growth from a small and predominantly black congregation into a multi-racial and international church. Due to his ideology – he also considered himself to be God – many consider him to be a cult leader. The golden keys to Father Divine's success were his absolute insistence on his own divinity and his extravagant demonstrations of the power of faith – the faith of him getting rich as fast as possible at the expense of everyone else. Wide-boy, Pastor Jones, quickly learned these lessons and began putting on his own displays of 'bullshit' healing.

In carefully contrived theatrical settings, Jones organised followers to spew up chicken livers claiming they were cancers, raised perfectly fit young people (made up to look like paralysed ancients) from wheelchairs and astounded his congregation with his 'mind-reading powers'. Jones had a photographic memory and had already begun detailed files on all his followers. In a nutshell, he was a master of mind control and an arch-manipulator.

Now flush with other folk's cash, Jones took his young family off for two years' 'missionary work' in Brazil. Here he met hardline Marxists and added a fresh dollop of communist philosophy to his gospel of social change through 'Christian love'. On the way back to America, he stopped off in British Guiana, soon to become the independent country of Guyana.

Back in the USA, everything had changed. His fight to unite black and white was no longer a single-handed struggle. For the first time, he heard Martin Luther King expound his vision of a future America where racism would no longer be an issue. But what made an even more powerful impact were the words of Malcolm Little aka 'Malcolm X', an ex-offender and now civil rights activist who asked, 'What has Christianity done for black people – except oppress them?' Malcolm X rejected Christian love and even eventually broke with the Nation of Islam. According to him, armed insurrection was the only answer. And in a country that was dominated by a vast majority of whites, for black people, this amounted to 'revolutionary suicide'.

Jones had learned the ropes, so to speak. He had dabbled in some form of Christianity or another along with hardline Marxism: the latter all about 'collectivism and egalitarianism', the ideology being one of sacrificing his or her life for the good of the collective. The fact that Marxist–Leninist regimes confiscated private businesses and landholdings is something that truly appealed to Jones at this time. The Vietnam War, Civil Rights marches in the South, and race riots across the USA, convinced Jones that he must take his followers to the 'Promised Land' – at least this was his excuse. And so this bigoted control freak started to preach this with a forked tongue. He was a power-hungry extreme narcissist and he saw that Martin Luther King and the rising Black Power Movement were a threat to him. He knew they would diminish his control over his ardent followers. Have I not written thus far in this book that narcissists and sociopaths/psychopaths thrive on being able to control others, of course I have, but what happens when they come undone? With Jones we shall see his reaction, being one of the most sickening in all of criminal history.

At first, he relocated the Peoples Temple in Redwood Valley, near Ukiah, California, bussing hundreds of his 'disciples' across the country. Some stayed behind. But those who went had to sell all their properties and give all of the proceeds to Rev. Jones. These people became totally dependent on him and the Temple. Yes, they had all been brainwashed.

From Redwood Valley, the Temple spread into San Francisco and Los Angeles. Jones opened food kitchens and day-care centres. Soon he was wielding political power. He could deliver his several thousand members as a block vote. Virtually every liberal office holder – from Lieutenant Governor of the State of California down to District Attorney – was offered the chance to address the congregation and they all quickly became beholden to Jones. San Francisco's Democrat Mayor, George Richard Moscone, courted him. Jones's powerbase was growing exponentially. Even national politicians cultivated relationships with him. During the 1976 presidential campaign, he had dinner with Rosalynn Carter who later occasionally wrote to him from the White House. Jones used his influence to secure preferential treatment for his congregation with welfare agencies, housing authorities, and even in court. Who would have thought that he would become one of the worst mass killers known to mankind?

While in California, Jones met an ambitious young lawyer named Timothy Oliver Stoen, who had just married his vivacious young wife, Grace Lucy Grech. Tim's book, *Marked for Death: My War with Jim Jones the Devil of Jonestown*, is a must-read, and a very disturbing one at that. Back then Stoen was disillusioned after the assassination of President J.F. Kennedy in 1963, and was searching for a revolutionary way ahead. The silver-tongued Jones promised just that. His multi-racial congregation and free-wheeling Christian/Marxist philosophy seemed to represent the wave of the future. Jones's political clout could also secure Stoen the plum job of Assistant DA in San Francisco – but there was a price to be paid.

They always say that there is no such thing as a free lunch, and the price of Stoen's participation was his wife. On 25 January 1972 she bore a son, John-John. Although the birth certificate lists Tim Stoen as the father, in a private affidavit Tim admitted that he had requested Jones to sire a child by his wife 'with the steadfast hope that said child will become the devoted follower of Jesus Christ and be instrumental in bringing God's kingdom here on earth, as has been his wonderful natural father.' And to think that Stoen had graduated from Wheaton College with a B.A. in political science later from Stanford Law School. What on earth was going through this allegedly intelligent man's mind? The affidavit was witnessed by Marceline – Jones's wife – Grace Stoen's feelings were not recorded and I am not a bit surprised.

Like so many sociopathic cult leaders, Jones was priapic. He used sex not just for pleasure but for power. He encouraged both sexes to sleep with him. This weakened the bond between married couples and bound both individuals closer to the Temple. Young women, even underage girls amongst his followers seemed to consider it a privilege to satisfy his sexual cravings. Jones was very like the now dead and very much in Hell, Jeffrey Epstein (both Jones and Epstein had very similar psychopathologies, needs and power cravings). Donald Trump is same-same in so many ways. An extreme narcissist, amoral bigot, born again liar, control freak, a self-opinionated dictatorial authoritarian, if one digs deep into the psychopathologies we see simple comparisons that are so easy to understand if we care to go look see.

One of Jones's secretaries kept a special appointments book for her boss's sexual dalliances. He openly boasted of his prowess, claiming almost superhuman potency, technique and endurance. At one time it is claimed that he even sought psychiatric advice on how to bring his libido under control, although I rather doubt that this is true. But now we can see much deeper into his mind, can we not?

In the Peoples Temple, no sex was allowed with outsiders – and any relationship inside the congregation needed the Temple's approval. Jones had at least three children by members of the congregation, though one woman had an abortion rather than bear his child. Sex was also frequently a topic of discussion at meetings of the all-important 'Planning Commission'. This was an inner circle of around a hundred members, largely the better-educated, middle-class whites. These meetings would drag on until the early hours. Jones would rail against bourgeois sexual attitudes and force members to confess publicly their sexual fears and fantasies, all of which was demeaning and allowed Jones to exert even more control over his 'flock'. Long periods of celibacy were sometimes demanded – not for Jones himself, of course – and sex was dubbed a 'revolutionary act' and one not to be indulged in for pleasure. What a disgusting bigot this man was! On one occasion, Jones coerced a white man into performing sex with a black woman during a meeting to prove that he was free of racial prejudice – but he never had sex with a black woman. Sexual frankness (read this as public nudity and public urination), Jones contended, were symbolic demonstrations of the community's openness. This was a congregation that could wander around urinating and defecating all over the place as long as it wasn't in Jones's own bed. It comes as no surprise that some members were disturbed by the pleasure Jones seemed to take in exhibiting himself in this blatant abuse of power.

While relationships were becoming more open and the community more of a sexual free-for-all, Jones was becoming increasingly paranoid which is not uncommon in extreme narcissists when they sense any loss of control. (Think Trump as his paranoia is exhibited in his rambling, almost incoherent tweets, as he finally realises that Biden is about to sit in the Oval Office). Yep, that should well and truly piss off the GOP and 'Trumpites', but I truly do love the US of A – allegedly!

Silly me, I digressed again for Jones's fears were sparked off, in part, by the defection of two long-term members. Elmer and Deanna Mertle had first visited the Peoples Temple in Redwood Valley as newlyweds in 1968. There they found a friendship and community they had not experienced before – it was Utopia and Jones immediately followed the Word of God – he enthusiastically fleeced them. They sold their home and just about everything they owned and moved into a farm Jones generously found for them. When I say 'farm', I mean a small plot of uncultivated land upon which sat not some splendid house complete with power and fresh water supplies, just a wooden hut made out of sheets of plywood and sod all else, and the Mertles were happy – yeah, I bet they were.

Within a few weeks, our philanthropic Rev. Jones had found them menial jobs, moreover, by 1975, the Mertles were members of the 'Planning Commission', but were becoming increasingly disturbed by Jones's bizarre behaviour. And, when he spanked their naked daughter for a minor infraction, they decided to leave. However, upping sticks was not as easy as they thought. Two of their children were living in the homes of other Temple members and they felt more commitment to Jones than to their natural parents. Their home and everything they owned belonged to the Temple – that is it belonged to Rev. Jones. They had been completely supported by – and surrounded by – the Temple for five years and had had little or no contact with the outside world, but help was at hand.

Elmer Mertle's mother was made of stern stuff, a battle-axe, an amply built lady of substantial means, she came to the rescue, giving them a profitable rest home she owned in Berkeley and cash to buy a house. However, when Deanna Mertle called one of Jones's aides to tell him they were leaving, a delegation came round and tried to persuade them to change their minds. When this failed, Jones threatened to smear Elmer as a child molester. The Mertles responded by threatening to go to the press. Jones was now mentally falling apart and the Mertles only extricated themselves from his grip by changing their names to Jeannie and Al Mills and placing documents damaging to the Temple and sworn affidavits charging Jones with all manner of indecent behaviour in a safe deposit box. Jones later claimed the Mertles had sold out their congregational 'brothers' and 'sisters, for a pocketful of credit cards and a fancy car.'

After this, defectors' houses were watched to make sure they were not talking to the authorities or to hostile journalists. In fact, at this time Jones's powerful political friends practically guaranteed that the claims of the defectors would be ignored.

Jones was convinced that his phone was being tapped by the FBI and that he was being followed by government agents. But underneath his paranoia, 'Dad' was getting ready to reveal his sinister hidden agenda publicly – though the world would not take a blind bit of notice.

On Memorial Day 1977, Reverend Jones was invited to speak to an anti-suicide rally in San Francisco. The half-witted purpose of the rally was to get the city fathers to construct an anti-suicide barrier along the Golden Gate Bridge – a favourite dropping off point for those with a wish to plunge 220 feet and get terminally and permanently wet. But here is the kicker... Jones's speech began with stern moral disapproval of suicide, but halfway through he lost the plot. To the amazement of all, his condemnation of suicide flipped and became a blanket endorsement of it. He had first mentioned the idea of 'revolutionary suicide' to Grace Stoen in 1973. At that time, he had only been planning for his followers to die. Most graciously, this public-spirited prophet would stay alive to explain *why* they had dunnit.

In 1976, he had carried out an experiment. On New Year's Day, he coerced his followers into drinking what he told them was poison. He railed against the 'traitors' who had left the Peoples Temple and told the congregation that they could only prove their loyalty to him by drinking the poison. As one might imagine, some became hysterical – and wouldn't you – but after the mock shooting of a member who *tried* to run away, Jones's followers meekly did what they were told. Forty-five minutes later, he told them that the 'poison' was innocuous. They actually thanked him for testing them – they were Americans after all. I am sure us Brits would have legged it as fast as our feet could take us, agreed?

This would prove to be the first of a series of suicide rehearsals that Jones called 'white nights'. Each time the congregation was told they were swallowing poison – they could never be sure that they were not. But gradually this brainwashing convinced them and they got used to the idea of laying down their lives for 'Dad', who by now was claiming, like 'Superman', to have come from another planet. Beam me up, Scottie!

In 1974, Jones had paid $1 million for a lease on 27,000 acres of jungle in Guyana. In 1976, it was still an experimental agricultural outpost, but in 1977 large amounts of building materials were shipped up-river to nearby Port Kaituma. Some 380 Temple members applied for visas and headed for Guyana. The next year, another seven hundred – including about 150 children – set off. The entry fee for Jones's utopia was to give everything they owned or earned over to the Temple aka Rev. Jim Jones aka Superman. Some of the adults travelling to Jonestown got drunk in the grog shops of Georgetown. The party continued on the boats up-river. Out of their tiny minds on hard liquor, one girl, full of rum, had a fling with one of the Guyanese boatmen. The vessels became floating knocking shops and when they all staggered ashore Jones was not best pleased. He went ape!

Once inside the compound at Jonestown, iron discipline was enforced. Not only had his congregation been taken up the river they'd been taken up 'Shit Creek' as well. Casual sexual encounters were banned and the 'Relationship Committee' enforced three months celibacy on any couple applying to have a serious and stable relationship. Such prohibitions did not apply to Rev. Superman of course. He moved into a hut – the best hut – with two of his mistresses while his wife lived nearby. One young girl who refused this pervert's advances was forcibly drugged and taken from the Jonestown 'hospital' to Jones's hut each night. Those who found his favour were given special privileges. For one example, the Jonestown doctor who supported Jones's claim that non-revolutionary sex caused cancer was indulged with a succession of teenage girls. And when one brave young woman left, Jones confessed that her defection was *his* fault because he had refused to have sex with her. He claimed that she wanted 'bourgeois sex' – for pleasure only – while, for him having sex in this socialist utopia was exclusively a political act. Yeah, right!

Beatings were commonplace for minor offences or simply because Jones thought a follower's 'head was between their legs' – that is, thinking about sexual matters instead of the 'mission's work' which included the growing of crops and corn in a move towards self-sufficiency. His spies were everywhere and he was especially hard on any man making advances to a woman he himself was attracted to. Adults were caned, forced to fight each other until 'right triumphed', or simply beaten into bloody submission. Children were informed on for minor breaches of discipline. They were taken before a microphone at 2 a.m. and beaten – as many as seventy-five times – while their cries echoed from the PA system around the compound. One child was buried in a metal box for twenty-four hours. Others were lowered down a well, where they were pulled into the water by a waiting assistant. This compound was Hell on Earth!

Meanwhile, Jones became increasingly more paranoid. He claimed to have killed a burglar breaking into his hut and served the man's flesh up in a stew for his followers. While his people toiled in the fields from sunrise to sunset, he stayed in his hut taking drugs and monitoring the news from San Francisco and the Temple's outpost in Georgetown. He controlled the community's listening and, even then, doctored all news from the outside world.

He claimed that Jonestown was about to be attacked by a force of mercenaries trained by the CIA who were mustering in a staging area across the Brazilian border. Soon they would attack, warned Jones. Armed guards were posted around the compound, ostensibly to protect the members of the Temple from attack. In truth, they were to prevent disaffected believers escaping from Rev. Jim Jones's 'utopia'. The end of the world was nigh! Holding high above his head the Holy Book, in his sunglasses he preached the impending apocalyptic, totally BS events that were soon to befall them all, one of his favourites being, Luke 21:25–26:

'And there will be signs in sun and moon and stars, and on the earth distress of nations in perplexity because of the roaring of the sea and the waves, people fainting with fear and foreboding of what is coming on the world. For the powers of the heavens will be shaken'.

Etcetera, *ad infinitum ad nauseum*.

On 8 November 1978, the Rev. Jim Jones sat on his crude wooden throne – yes he had a throne – deep in the jungles of Guyana, South America. He had bad news for his 1,000 followers. Most of them were about to die. What he didn't reveal was the truth. A support group, the 'Committee of Concerned Relatives', had been formed to publicise the facts about the Peoples Temple. One of these relatives, Sam Houston, a journalist with the Associated Press, accused the cult of murdering his son, who had left the Temple after a violent argument with Jones. The next day, the lad had died in a grisly railroad accident near the waterfront in San Francisco. The truth was that the lad had actually committed suicide.

Nevertheless, one of Houston's drinking pals was Democrat congressman, Leo Joseph Ryan. Several of the Temple's members came from Ryan's congressional district in south San Francisco. Houston persuaded Ryan to investigate the sect and find out exactly what was going on in the Temple's South American settlement of Jonestown.

On 24 October 1978, Ryan received authorisation from the House Foreign Affairs Committee to go to Guyana. With legal action threatening to cut off the sect's American funds, Jones had no choice but to allow him to visit but tried to lay down conditions. He said he would not allow Ryan into Jonestown if he brought any 'traitors' or the press with him but the feisty, silver-haired congressman would have none of this. He turned up in Guyana with four members of the Committee of Concerned Relatives, reporters and photographers from the San Francisco dailies, the *Washington Post* and an NBC film crew. Fifty-three-year-old Leo Ryan had researched race riots and studied prison reform before turning his attention to Jonestown. Greg Robinson was a *San Francisco Examiner* photographer. Thirty-six-year-old Robert Brown, the NBC cameraman, ironically shot a minute-by-minute recording of what would prove to become his own last hours on earth. Only a fifty-nine-minute film survives. A pensive, tight-lipped and obviously furious, Jones is filmed wearing a red sweatshirt and sunglasses. The little boy in the brown and yellow striped sweatshirt is John-John, Jones's son. He too would soon die. The reader can find this unedited NBC archive footage of Jonestown on the internet. It *will* bring tears to your eyes – it did to mine because it is heartbreaking to think that the only thing these innocent men, women and children ever wanted was a happy life. Bless them. The first part of this archive material stops after the concert because just as the group were about to board their aircraft they were all gunned down.

It is now completely impossible for me to add any more words to this account of Jim Jones. The case is a fascinating one. As you will see from the NBC footage, there are those who hate this preacher man while others idolised him. So I ask you to form your own opinion of who he was, where he was at, and why he did what he did – to finally shoot himself in the head with hundreds of his loving followers dying in agony around him. Does Jim Jones deserve a very special place in Hell? You, dear reader, can figure this out for yourself.

★★★

Conclusion

It seems fitting that as I pen these last words, it just happens to be Friday, 13 November 2020 – the day that the death of Peter Sutcliffe in prison was announced. An auspicious date indeed.

My brief for this book was to figure out who, in my humble opinion, the ten most heinous serial killers/mass murderers of all time are – those that really deserve a special place in Hell. It's an almost impossible task as we *all* have our own views regarding levels of evil and those who transcend evil. No doubt there will be critics who say that I have missed the worst of the worst, but then, if they are so inclined, I welcome them to write their own book, bless them, and let the devil take the hindmost.

I rest my case.
Enjoy and no nightmares please.

★★★